Nyack Sketch Log

AN ARTIST AND WRITER EXPLORES
THE HISTORY OF A HUDSON RIVER VILLAGE

BURD

Nyack Sketch Log

AN ARTIST AND WRITER EXPLORES THE HISTORY OF A HUDSON RIVER VILLAGE

SKETCHES AND SHORT ESSAYS BY BILL BATSON

Foreword by Art Gunther III

Preface by Sabrina Weld Feldman

Introduction by Bill Batson

Published by Bill Batston Arts Ltd.
billbatsonarts.com

Nyack Sketch Log:
An Artist and Writer Explores the History of a Hudson River Village
Essays and illustrations by Bill Batson
Foreword by Art Gunther III
Preface by Sabrina Weld Feldman

ISBN 978-0-692-32114-0

First edition

Book design by Loraine Machlin
Typeset in Minion and Frutiger

Printed in the United States of America

Dedicated to the memory of my father, William Prime Batson

Contents

Preface

Bill Batson gives a resonating voice to the lives, the history, and the architecture that make our community so extraordinary. As a company dedicated to building community, Weld Realty is proud to be a partner of such a talented wordsmith and illustrator. Bill's *Nyack Sketch Log* weaves the disparate threads of past and present lives into our shared story of Nyack, which will unite us for generations to come.

There is something enchanting about reading the secret histories tucked away in plain sight. Over a century of love, quarrels, art, dreams, fame, and revolution linger behind the picturesque corbels and shutters of our riverfront town. And Bill Batson reveals these secret histories to us, one fascinating, vividly illustrated tale at a time.

Thank you, Bill, for giving such a profound gift of storytelling to your community and for preserving for posterity what may have otherwise been lost.

Sabrina Weld Feldman
Real Estate Broker/President
Weld Realty
Nyack, N. Y.

WELD
REALTY

Foreword

In every age there is a town crier, someone who chronicles the life of a community, who gathers the facts and then reports the news. The best of these public reporters bring you to the heart of the matter right away, knowing that your attention is pulled in every direction. When the town crier can immediately capture a reader's attention, present the facts but also entertain, while enticing the reader to stay longer, then you have a master writer.

Such a scribe is Bill Batson, who has written the *Nyack Sketch Log* in such quantity, with such breadth of fact and depth of understanding, that he has become a treasure in Nyack and throughout New York's Rockland County.

Each week Bill assigns himself varied topics, ranging from the arts, local culture, and rich history of Rockland and Nyack, to village regulars and wonderful street characters, stores, businesses, and organizations, each with compelling stories to tell. A visit with Bill Batson and his weekly column is like meeting an old friend for a long, leisurely, informative, most entertaining lunch.

Bill gives us images to ponder as well. His line drawings of Concklin's Barn, Edward Hopper's house, old homes, and so much of the landscape, shout out, "Hey, man, take a look at this place, this person." We are then hooked by prose and artwork.

Since Bill is also a longtime activist on behalf of bettering the human condition, the writer/artist offers a sensitive, tasteful, and respectful-of-our-views sales pitch. We do not have to accept it, or even part of his movement and bent, but in the end, if truth be told, we are a bit seduced by his logic.

In a quieter, slower-paced age, even going back to the humbling, informative traditions of our Native Americans, our immigrant ancestors, our great-grandparents of every ethnic background and culture, there were the storytellers, passing along fact, fiction, fable, acquired wisdom, lessons in living, standards to exist by, examples of endurance, and hope for the future, no matter how cloudy a particular day may be. Bill Batson is a modern storyteller and his words, his art, his topics, the rhythm of his prose, and the slant of his ink pen gather us to a warming hearth, before a fire, in coziness and revelation. We beg for more and tarry awhile, though our *iPhones* and *Twitter* messages may try to lure us away. They cannot, for the *Nyack Sketch Log* moment can be magnetic.

Communities everywhere throughout the world have had chroniclers like Bill, and despite the decline of traditional print media, they always will, since people will forever thirst for information and stories about everything, and the understanding of it all, too. In the here and now, in this Nyack and Rockland County of ours, we have our town crier, Bill Batson, and we are richer for that.

Please savor and enjoy this collection of short essays and sketches meant to be re-read and re-read.

Art Gunther III
The Edward Hopper House Art Center trustee, retired editorial page editor, Journal News
Blauvelt, N.Y.

Introduction

The unexamined place is not worth inhabiting. I am fascinated with every building and every soul that dwells within the one-square-mile village where I live. Each person's story is a poem, a screenplay, a song, that has yet to be written, seen, or heard.

I started crafting a composite portrait of Nyack after meeting Kris Burns. Kris is the artist-in-residence of the Edward Hopper House Art Center, the converted childhood home of Nyack's visual arts hero. On June 18, 2011, I watched how she transformed the village into a living Hopper painting with the public art tools of flash mobs and pop-up projections. Her event, *Hopper Happens*, had a profound impact on me.

There was something about the projection of an Edward Hopper painting on the side of a brick wall that made the village that I had known all my life new again. Suddenly every facade was as captivating as a distant, exotic locale. Vistas that had become mundane were now begging for my attention.

That night I met Dave Zornow, publisher of *NyackNewsAndViews.com*. In the weeks after our meeting, Dave saw me sitting on curbs around town drawing buildings. He asked me to submit an example of my work with a short caption. My caption was 750 words. The *Nyack Sketch Log* was born.

Nyack Sketch Log is grown-up show and tell. Each week I publish a sketch and short essay that explores a local person or place of interest. Since August, 2011, I have made 165 Sketch Log entries. My column has over 100,000 page views. This book presents some of my favorites.

I don't write just to boast about the abundance of intriguing people and places in Nyack. I write to defend my community, my neighbors, and to rally others to the cause. I am using my keyboard and my pen to promote preservation, cultural literacy, tolerance, and community empowerment.

Hyper local art and journalism can heighten our awareness of our surroundings: of the beauty of the built and natural environment, of the extraordinary life stories of people we pass every day, of the value of having public spaces and markets and town squares, and of the unique character of places that have been collectively constructed by preceeding generations. If we become more observant of our environment and our community, we might become more aware of its needs and more zealous in its defense.

So yes, I believe that any place becomes more habitable if examined. But the truth is some places are more worthy of habitation than others. The people, the history, the culture, the small businesses, the natural features, the diversity make this place, in my mind, the finest stretch along the Hudson. My sketches and short essays form my argument that there is no spot sweeter than Nyack.

Bill Batson,
December, 2014

Nyack Sketch Log

AN ARTIST AND WRITER EXPLORES
THE HISTORY OF A HUDSON RIVER VILLAGE

BURD
ST.

Warts and All

In 1884, Nyack, N.Y. was a bustling river community and the commercial heart of Rockland County. This sketch, based on a widely circulated map, *Nyack on the Hudson*, made by L. R. Burleigh in that year, depicts a jumble of homes, businesses, and churches. I recently took a closer look at this historical document and discovered that our 19th-century republic on the Hudson was not as indivisible as the promise made in our pledge of allegiance.

The 1884 map has a legend that designated 42 places of interest, including ten churches. Eight of the churches are identified by denomination; the last two are listed by sect and by race. When I noticed this detail for the first time, it took my breath away. St. Philip's African Methodist Episcopal Church, which stands today on the corner of North Mill and Burd Streets, was listed in the legend as "Zion's M.E. Church (Colored)." The church, now known as Pilgrim Baptist, located at the corner of High Avenue and Franklin Street, was identified as "Second Baptist Church (Colored)."

"We honor the progress our society has made when we publish the unvarnished map of 1884, warts and all."

Twenty years ago, I traveled to rural Georgia to help a legal team exonerate a death row inmate named Curfew Davis. Needing the exact street address of a Baptist Church where we were expected for a meeting, I called information. When I asked the operator for the listing, in a deadpan drawl, she surprised me with her own question: she wanted to know which Baptist Church I was looking for. I told her I did not know. She asked again and I got her drift. Even though it was 1990, the ghost of Jim Crow ran through the phone and down my spine. "The black one," I replied.

I felt the same chill when I noticed the legend on the 1884 map. Was the distinction "colored" made as a boast, a proud assertion that the village accommodated two black churches? Was it a warning to prevent someone from walking into a congregation of clashing complexion, or something more ominous?

I was more saddened than shocked when I confronted the legacy of segregation in the South in the 1990s. I knew that the removal of overt signs of discrimination, like those posted on water fountains and bathrooms in the 1960s, hadn't ended racism, but it was sobering to consider that members of the same religious denomination still required separate houses of worship for each race.

My great-grandfather, George T. Avery, was a spokesperson for the black community and a member of Zion's M.E. Church at the time this map was drawn. From our vantage point today, the notation "colored" is an awkward relic of past discrimination. For the members of these two churches, the fact that the distinction was made in such a public fashion was of enormous social and material consequence.

A more noble aspect of our democracy is that we keep these ugly details of our evolution in our documents. We do not pretend that the abhorrent customs of American apartheid never existed. We resist the temptation to destroy the evidence of our troubled past.

You do not need to read far into the Constitution to be reminded that when apportioning congressional seats, black people were counted as three fifths of a person. It would be a profound injustice if some well-meaning printer sanitized copies of the Constitution, or the map of 1884, and removed these examples of racial discord. We honor the progress our society has made, the burdens of people like my great-grandfather and the members of St. Philip's and Pilgrim, when we publish the unvarnished map of 1884, warts and all.

batson 8-3-11

AUGUST 23, 2011

Liberty Street

This house and this street are the remnants of Nyack's oldest middle-class black neighborhood. In the early 20th century, a group of African-American families bought homes in Nyack. Home ownership by blacks in Nyack was a stunning achievement when you consider the fact that merely 50 years earlier blacks owned nothing: blacks were owned!

The speed of this reversal in fortune is hard to comprehend. In historic terms, 50 years is a tiny interval. Fifty years ago was 1961. Imagine a family advancing from slavery to home ownership in the time span that America went from black-and-white TV to digital cable. My 60s reference is purposeful irony. It was a time of urban renewal, a phenomenon of that era that destroyed the middle-class black community that many refer to as Jackson Avenue. Almost obliterated, that is, except for this house on Liberty Street.

My great-grandparents purchased the house on Jackson Avenue. My grandmother used the meager sum that she got through the condemnation process of the eminent domain debacle to buy another home. The only saving grace is that this site now holds much needed affordable housing and a senior citizen development.

As I sat on the ground in front of this modest structure and drew, a parking enforcement officer walked toward me. I asked him if he was going to ticket me for squatting in a parking space. He laughed and said if that was the case, he would have written me up weeks ago having seen me numerous times perched on the curbside drawing. I think he chose this moment to say hello because he approved of my subject matter. It turned out that he knew my aunt, who was once the Deputy Village Clerk and who grew up on Jackson Avenue.

I was then approached by a local artist who told me she admires but avoids representational drawings. She is an abstract painter, which I told her I envy. She lamented the demands of linear perspective, telling me how she would throw in the towel after the first line went astray. Watching my imprecise and quivering depiction, she thought aloud that if she could have forgiven herself the occasional errant mark, she would have seen that the whole is greater than the sum of its imperfect parts.

Because I draw freehand with black ink on white paper, I confront the fear of failure with every pen stroke. Yet, I persist and complete each drawing, motivated by my attachment to the village and enriched by my random interactions with the villagers. That someone who loves Nyack and is making art would consider drawing from life after meeting me on this special site was invigorating. During this encounter, I could feel the freedom that my ancestors must have felt on this spot. As modest as this home appears, its very existence and hidden history is profound and I am pleased to have archived it. The cartographers got this one right. Liberty Street is aptly named.

"Imagine a family advancing from slavery to home ownership in the time span that America went from black and white TV to digital cable."

BATSON 2012

St. Philip's A.M.E. Zion Church

Two years before Abraham Lincoln was sworn in as president, St. Philip's A.M.E. Zion Church was founded in 1859 by abolitionist John W. Towt. Today, the term abolitionist is considered a badge of honor. In the 1850s, as slave catchers roamed the north empowered by the loathsome Fugitive Slave Act, the title brought legal jeopardy and mortal danger. It was under the gathering and ominous clouds of a civil war over race-based slavery that Towt arrived in Nyack, determined to contribute to the welfare of the black community.

In 1821, the 19-year-old white Methodist was exposed to the cruel perversion of slavery while traveling through the south. Towt settled in Nyack in 1859 after a successful career in New York City where he amassed a fortune. He immediately threw himself into the effort to ensure that there was a Sunday school for black children in the village. At the same time he made arrangements to secure property for a church building and accommodations for a minister.

"From its inception the AME Zion Church was an active participant in the Underground Railroad, counting Harriet Tubman, Frederick Douglass, and Sojourner Truth as members."

It is not surprising that the church that Towt would help establish was of the African Methodist Episcopal Zion denomination; the A.M.E. Zion Church was founded in New York City in 1796. From its inception, the church was an active participant in the Underground Railroad and counted Harriet Tubman, Frederick Douglass, and Sojourner Truth as members.

Though Towt played many roles in the congregation, including superintendent of the Sunday school, the day-to-day operation and religious activities of the church were led by members and pastors of African descent. The enduring wooden edifice at the corner of Burd and North Mill Streets is evidence of the prudence and probity of the congregation.

At a meeting in early 1886, the chairman of the building committee, William H. Myers, argued against repairing the church and asked all those in favor of building a new church to stand. The whole congregation rose to his challenge. My great-grandfather, George T. Avery, was one of those who stood up. As the Chairman of the Board of Trustees, he contributed $36 towards the $2,311 that was eventually raised. The building, dedicated on Sunday, December 17, 1886, was of such solid design and durable material that it still stands.

Mr. Towt made his last public appearance in the pulpit of St. Philip's on September 11, 1887. He was said to have been pleased with the results of his 28 years of collaboration with Nyack's black community. He told those assembled that, as its founder, he felt doubly repaid by the fact that his efforts had not been in vain.

Four generations of my family attended St. Philip's: my great-grandfather, George T. Avery; his daughter, Frances Lillian Avery Batson, who was a Secretary of the Trustee Board; my aunt, the former Deputy Clerk for the Village of Nyack, Frances Adeline Batson; my cousin, Sylvia Peterson; and me.

Few buildings celebrate 153 anniversaries. Even fewer organizations reach such an august milestone. The spirit of those who endured slavery and those who risked their lives, freedom, and property to abolish the barbaric institution survive through the longevity of St. Philip's A.M.E. Zion Church. Like an eternal flame, the ideas of freedom and self-determination that John W. Towt enshrined in this humble wooden building have been diligently tended by generations of members of the St. Philip's family. May they never be extinguished.

1967
5727
ESTABLISHE
1891

SEPTEMBER 23, 2014

Congregation Sons of Israel

In accordance with the Hebrew calendar, synagogues welcomed the year 5775 on September 24, 2014. As congregations ponder the passage of time and seek edification from the stories that inform their faith, a document published in 1991 by Congregation Sons of Israel offers a detailed and intimate account of the history of the Jewish community in Nyack.

Written and edited by Myra Dembrow, *From Generation to Generation, One Hundred Years of Jewish Life in Nyack*, provides a splendid and sweeping glimpse into the formation of the congregation that now worships on North Broadway in Upper Nyack. Dembrow describes the late-19th-century village that attracted itinerant Jewish peddlers from New York City as "a bustling center of commerce at the intersection of the only two roads that completely cross Rockland County, the roads that are now known as Route 9W and Route 59."

"Gert Goldstein Mages recalled being the only Jewish girl at Liberty School in 1914. When prayers were read, Goldstein was sent to stand in the hall."

In March of 1870, a space in Abraham Brown's tailor shop on Main Street in Nyack became the meeting place for the Jewish Society of Nyack. On August 22, 1891, that group incorporated as the Congregation of Nyack, B'nai Israel.

Gert Goldstein Mages recalled being the only Jewish girl at Liberty School in 1914. When prayers were read, Goldstein was sent to stand in the hall.

On March 2, 1920, the congregation acquired a parcel of land next to the library from Tunis Depew for $100. After four years of fundraising, a cornerstone was laid at the corner of Hudson Avenue and South Broadway. The building was completed in 1925.

When the congregation changed its name to Sons of Israel in 1936, the Jewish community in Rockland County was still so small that congregant Charles Barracks claimed he knew every member.

In 1955, a group held separate Yom Kippur services at a nearby church hall. Even though the rancor died down, a fault line that would eventually become a full-blown schism had emerged. The 1960s were a period of social activism around issues of racial justice in America. In the 19th century, a bond was built between Congregation Sons of Israel and the African-American community in Nyack. In the 1860s, founding members Abraham Brown and Moses Oppenheimer were active in the Underground Railroad. One hundred years later, in February 1963, 70 members of St. Philip's A.M.E. Zion Church were invited to worship at Sons of Israel in a race relations Sabbath. On a following Sunday, Reverend McKinney invited Rabbi Krantz and his congregation to a service at St. Philip's.

In much of the country, the 1960s were a time of tumultuous change, with trends sometimes going in contradictory directions. For Sons of Israel, plans to obtain a new building reopened an old rift, eventually creating Nyack's second synagogue, Temple Beth Torah.

In June 1964, having outgrown their aging temple on South Broadway and Hudson Avenue, the congregation sold the building to Berea Seventh Day Adventist Church for $70,000. A property on North Broadway in Upper Nyack was acquired, the colonial-style mansion on the site was demolished, and new construction was undertaken.

While construction was being completed, services were temporarily held in a carriage house on the property that was converted into a house of worship by congregation member and owner of Rockland County's largest construction firm, Harry Degenshein. At noon on December 19, 1965, a motorcade brought the sacred Torah scroll from Hudson Avenue to the new synagogue.

The John Towt House

Imagine the stories that would be told if houses wrote autobiographies. This stately structure on South Highland Avenue could tell us if slaves were hidden here during the abolition movement. The garden could share the secrets of what makes her bloom. But alas, buildings and garden beds don't write books. Fortunately for us, this house has a biographer and her name is Judy Martin.

"Imagine the stories that would be told if houses wrote autobiographies."

If someone wanted to create a biography of their house, where would they start?

You start with the land, its earliest ownership records, and historical maps. I went to the county clerk's office and researched the deeds as far back as I could go. Deeds follow the actual ownership of the land and show changes, liens, and court records. If it's a recent building, the municipal building department has pertinent records. And once you have the deeds, you can check the names to see who those people were.

The earliest owner that is documented, John Towt, was rumored to be an abolitionist. Are there any cavities in the home where escaping slaves could have hidden?

There were several places to hide a runaway slave in the old house, and there may have been more that were lost when spaces were taken for the indoor plumbing installation.

On the 4th floor there was a floor-to-ceiling wardrobe and a walk-in cedar closet. On the 3rd floor was a three-part bay window seat that opened, and a hallway between rooms with doors opening out on each side.

Connecting the 2nd floor and the bottom floor kitchen there was a dumbwaiter, controlled entirely by ropes and pulleys inside the shaft, and located right next to an exit door on the second floor. And on the bottom floor there was a closet/exit door leading to the coal bin and a highly unusual small window leading from the underground root/fruit cellar to the space under the porch.

What drew you to this house?

When we walked on Main Street in Nyack, people we did not know greeted us, just as in our upstate village. The first time we saw the house was on a foggy evening. We put in an offer and it was accepted, without ever knowing the house had a 12 month Hudson River view. The house was one of a kind, which appealed to us, and finally, we could afford it. It had 12 rooms, and every one of those and every inch outside needed help!

What's your favorite room in the house?

I love to cook and I love to eat so, of course, the kitchen is my favorite place. But for a quiet time with a good book the house has lots of cozy corners and window seats and bay windows. And if it's a really good thunder and lightning storm, you'll find us outside on the porch, loving it!

It seems that you put as much effort into the grounds as you do the building. What is your favorite feature in your garden?

Up by the house, the hydrangeas, azaleas, and rhododendrons create lovely living walls against which annuals smile at the house. But the private place is the terrace, totally surrounded by green and supporting perennials changing with the seasons.

What is your current garden project?

I've just finished harvesting the mint to make mint jelly for lamb and curry dinners all winter.

UNDERGRO
RAILROAD
UGRR

MAY 15, 2013

Underground Railroad

Joseph Mitlof erected a shrine and several historic markers to the Underground Railroad in Nyack. For Mitlof, who passed away in April 2014, the telling of the story of the Underground Railroad was not just an effort to preserve history, but an opportunity to celebrate an event that he believed "epitomizes the concept of people helping other people."

A shroud of secrecy surrounded the actions of the men and women who provided aid to escaping slaves before 1863 when slavery was abolished. It was the notorious clandestine nature of the network of safe houses, called stations, that made me stop in my tracks when I saw the words Underground Railroad in large black letters on the side of Mitlof's structure. The shockingly incongruent signage had served its purpose. I was reminded that Nyack was an important stop on the route that escaping slaves took to reach freedom in Canada. And my appetite had been whetted to learn more.

"It is widely held that Nyack was the midpoint between two locations on the Underground Railroad: Jersey City, 39 miles to our south, and Newburgh, 40 miles to our north."

In 1827, slavery was abolished in New York State. According to noted historian, Carl Nordstrum, there was a substantial free black community in Nyack by 1850. Arriving in Rockland County should have been the equivalent of reaching the Promised Land for fleeing bondsmen. However, aiding an escaping slave was a crime on either side of the Mason Dixon line. The Fugitive Slave Act, passed in 1793 and expanded in 1850, allowed bounty hunters, known as "blackbirders," to roam the country seizing people of color for return to the South regardless of whether they were escaped slaves.

It is widely held that Nyack was the midpoint between two locations on the Underground Railroad: Jersey City, 39 miles to our south, and Newburgh, 40 miles to our north. In a contemporary account of the secret sanctuary movement published in 1886, Dr. Frank B. Green confirmed Nyack as a stop on the Underground Railroad. He also mentioned names of families who were known to be involved in the clandestine activity, including the Hesdras and the Towts.

The first marker that Mitlof helped erect was unveiled on Presidents' Day in 2002. In his capacity as the group's historian, Mitlof convinced the American Legion to fund the project on the site of the Hesdra house. The home of freed slave, Cynthia Hesdra, and her husband, Edward, stood at the corner of Route 59 and Route 9W. It was destroyed by order of the Urban Renewal Agency of Nyack in 1977, despite the objections of the Historical Society of the Nyacks and Village Trustee, Noel Oursler.

Giles R. Wright, the official black historian of the State of New Jersey, relies on five criteria for verifying an Underground Railroad site: the age of the building, its location, the ownership during the years the Underground Railroad was operating, oral history, and the rare written document. Mitlof did not suggest that his converted garage, which was located in a parking lot between Catherine and Main Streets just below Midland Avenue that has since been demolished, was an actual Underground Railroad location.

However, Mitlof's placement of markers meet some of the Giles Wright test: near the Hesdra house; St. Philip's, the church founded by abolitionist John W. Towt; and along the route of the Nyack Brook, which was used as a landmark for escaping slaves. More importantly, Mitlof's efforts have given inspiration to a current generation of historians who are working to permanently commemorate the sacrifice and courage of the men and women who built and operated an underground railroad.

Cynthia Hesdra Way
DEPEW AVE
PIERMONT AVE

Scholar Puts History on Map

Dr. Lori Martin helped erect this street sign that honors the memory of Cynthia Hesdra. When she published *The Ex-Slave's Fortune: The Story of Cynthia Hesdra* in 2008, Martin saved an important figure in local history from obscurity. Martin's work is a testimonial to the awesome riches inherent in knowledge. Through her teaching, and a growing bibliography, Dr. Martin wants to share the wealth.

"We all have a responsibility to be historical detectives, whether it is for our families or our communities."

Martin, a proud product of Nyack's public schools, believes "we all have a responsibility to be historical detectives, whether it is for our families or our communities." This intrepid and inquisitive spirit led her to uncover the story of Cynthia Hesdra.

In 2009, the quadricentennial of Henry Hudson's voyage up the Hudson River, Martin was asked to draft a report on the economic contribution of blacks during the last 400 years by Dr. Susan G. and Dr. Edmund W. Gordon of the CEJJES Institute. Her findings were to be presented to an assembly of Rockland County middle school students at Rockland Community College.

"Most of the research that I do involves pouring through census data, it doesn't involve getting into the lives of real people. But once I started doing the research for this project, I kept coming across the Hesdra name. I became curious about the mentions of Edward Hesdra and that Cynthia was curiously absent," she described.

The fact that Edward overshadowed Cynthia was inexplicable to Martin, because according to her trained eye, it was Cynthia that amassed all the wealth that the Hesdra family accumulated.

Cynthia Hesdra was born on March 6, 1808, in Tappan. Her father, John Moore, owned mills along the Hudson. At some point in her life, through a chain of events that is unclear, Cynthia was enslaved. She managed to not only win her freedom but she went on to operate businesses in Nyack and New York City and to own properties in New York and New Jersey.

"What was striking about Cynthia was her ability, and the ability of many other people of African ancestry, to move from being assets to asset owners," Martin observed.

When Cynthia Hesdra died on February 9, 1879, she was reportedly worth $100,000, the equivalent of $3 million in contemporary dollars. Allegations of fraud and forgery in the dispensation of her will against her husband Edward led to the first application of a law that compared known and disputed signatures in New York.

The Hesdra home stood at the corner of Route 9W and Route 59. The house was destroyed by order of the Urban Renewal Agency of Nyack in 1977, despite the objections of the Historical Society of the Nyacks. A historic marker on the spot mentions only Edward.

Cynthia and Edward Hesdra are listed in Mary Ellen Snodgrass's *Underground Railroad Encyclopedia* as conductors.

In August 2013, Martin took a position as Associate Professor at Louisiana State University. Her recent publications include, *Black Asset Poverty and the Enduring Racial Divide* and *Out of Bounds: Racism and the Black Athlete*, a collection of essays that explores how racial ideologies are created and recreated in all areas of public life, including the world of sports.

JANE
E.
GULFIELD
DIED
AUG 24
1884
AGED 13
3 MOS 15 DYS
SUSAN
O.
GULFIELD
DIED
JULY 24 1884
AGED
21 YRS 5 MOS 24 DYS
SAMUEL GULFIELD
A PRIVATE COR
25TH REGT. NY.
DIED MAY 18 1886
AGED 55 YRS 7 MOS 4 DAYS
AT REST
GULFIELD
RAISON

Mount Moor Cemetery

Cemeteries were segregated in America until the mid-20th century. Today, Mount Moor Cemetery stands as a monument to the twisted logic of racial discrimination. But the cemetery of approximately 90 veterans and civilians, located in West Nyack, also serves as a symbol of perseverance and defiance. The gravestones at Mount Moor endure, despite the initial efforts of the developers of the Palisades Mall to obliterate the burial ground.

Hezekiah Easter Jr. became the first African American elected to public office in Rockland County when he won a seat on the Village of Nyack Board of Trustees in 1965. His connection to Mount Moor Cemetery was deeply personal. In 1945, he helped bury his brother Linwood, who died from a ruptured appendix at age 15. His father, Hezekiah Easter Sr., a World War I veteran who owned a wood yard near the cemetery, was buried there in 1986. If the developers of the Palisades Mall had had their way, Hezekiah Easter Sr. would have been the last burial at Mount Moor.

"If the developers of the Palisades Mall had had their way, Hezekiah Easter, Sr. would have been the last burial at Mount Moor."

James and Jane Benson deeded the land that became Mount Moor Cemetery to William H. Moore, Stephen Samuels, and Isaac Williams on July 7, 1849. The land was purchased for the purpose of creating a non-denominational final resting place for black families that were excluded from cemeteries where whites were buried. The name of the cemetery captures the rugged topography of the location and the language of racial exclusion. The property is a wedge-shaped parcel on a steep hill and the term Moor was commonly used in the 15th through the 19th centuries to describe people of African descent.

In 1940, a group of leading African American Rocklanders established the Mount Moor Cemetery Association to maintain the burial ground. The first president was Reverend William Clyde Taylor, pastor of Pilgrim Baptist Church. In 1977, Hezekiah Easter Jr., who had been elected to the Rockland County Legislature in 1970, became President of the Association.

Easter's tenure as President of the Mount Moor Cemetery Association coincided with the beginning of the battle against over-development chronicled in the documentary film *Mega Mall*. A Syracuse, New York-based developer, the Pyramid Companies, announced their plan to build the second largest shopping mall in America next door to the cemetery in 1985. Proposals from the company included burying the plots under 100 feet of soil or disinterring the bodies for reburial elsewhere.

Aided by Jacqueline L. Holland, Leonard Cooke, Wilbur Folkes, Charlene Dunbar, Bea Fountain, and attorney Alicia Crowe, Easter stood firm. "We were not going to allow them to disturb these rightful resting places in order to accommodate more parking spaces," Crowe recalled.

At a meeting at Depew Manor in 1994, a representative of the Pyramid Companies surrendered to the group's demands. Once it was granted a place on the Federal Register, the cemetery could not be buried or dug up. There would also be one final tombstone.

On March 13, 2007, Hezekiah Easter Jr. was laid to rest beside his brother and his father. The man who saved the cemetery is the last man buried at Mount Moor. A parking structure and the facades of big-box stores loom in the distance, held at bay by a soldier and statesman who will forever keep his silent and solemn vigil over this hallowed ground.

50

Nyack Historical Society

Win Perry can measure his Hudson Valley heritage in centuries. "My ancestors have been farmers and boat builders and were descended from the earliest European settlers in Rockland County," Perry told me recently. As President of the Historical Society of the Nyacks for the last 12 years, Perry works tirelessly to commemorate the heritage of all the families that call the Nyacks home. This building that houses Nyack's Historical Society bears witness to the depth of Perry's connection to the village and reminds us of the benefits of historic preservation to the future well-being of our community.

The Historical Society operates from the ground floor of the Depew House, located on the corner of Piermont and Hudson Avenues, behind the Nyack Library. The Italianate-style, house was built between 1850 and 1851 by Peter Depew. The ample covered front porch overlooked green houses that the Depew family operated in what is now Memorial Park.

In a speech given in 1860, Captain Isaac P. Smith recalled his own childhood in 1814 when Nyack consisted of just seven houses. In Captain Smith's account, three of those houses were owned by the Tallmans and one by the Depews. One branch of Perry's family began when Uriah Perry arrived in the 1750s, another line can be traced to the Tallmans. Harman Tallman was the first European-born settler in Nyack and Rockland County, arriving in 1676.

Perry may have inherited his dedication to the public service that is historic preservation from his mother. She was a schoolteacher who went on to work for a Rockefeller family foundation where she helped start the Colonial Williamsburg Project in Virginia. Before joining the Historical Society Board, Perry, who is an architect by trade and historian by passion, described his work on the preservation of the Edward Hopper House in the 1970s as one of the greatest adventures of his life.

The Historical Society of the Nyacks was launched through an invitation published in *The Rockland Journal News* by Upper Nyack resident, Florence Katzenstein, on March 1, 1994. Katzenstein, who became the Society's first president, now heads the events and fundraising committee. The group has published six books, a quarterly newsletter, and has launched popular house tours and lecture programs.

In 2005, the Historical Society partnered with the Nyack Library to publish Carl Nordstrom's account of three centuries of race relations titled *Nyack in Black and White.* In 2009, documents gathered by Dr. Lori Martin that chronicled the role of African Americans in the history of the village were included in the exhibit, *Fish and Ships.* The inclusion of Dr. Martin's research coincided with the publication of her book, *The Ex-Slave's Fortune: The Story of Cynthia D. Hesdra.*

Items on display in the historical society museum include a piano made by the Tallman Factory and two Wilcox and Gibbs sewing machines. Perry was able to make available a small, green, reed organ that was in storage in his barn. The instrument was used in the St. Paul's Lutheran Church that now houses the Elmwood Playhouse.

Historic preservation is not an esoteric luxury but an invaluable tool in helping a community honor past achievements and avoid past mistakes. Restoring and preserving landmarks, like the Hopper House, for instance, can also provide more immediate benefits. Communities around the region are scrambling to attract consumers and tourists. When we treasure our history, we are also helping to secure our future.

"Historic preservation is not an esoteric luxury but an invaluable tool in helping a community honor past achievements and avoid past mistakes."

50 Piermont Avenue
Suite L-2, Nyack

Save Our Green House

The man who built this house, with the benefits from slave labor, laid much of the foundation for the village we occupy. Since his death in 1842, John Green's house has had many owners and tenants. Because of the neglect of its current absentee landlord, the building might soon crumble into dust.

John Edward Green was born in 1772. After a fire consumed his lumber business in Coeymans, N.Y., he arrived in Nyack to start from scratch. His first job was as a laborer for the Cornelison family. Soon he returned to the timber trade, opening his second lumberyard, around 1810.

Green built the house that now slumps behind chain-link fencing and barbed wire at the bottom of Main Street in 1819. It still exhibits the distinct traditional Dutch Colonial design with roughly-coursed stone walls (now covered in stucco) and a high gambrel roof. The sandstone used for the walls was quarried a few miles north. Some of the original stones are visible through a gaping hole on the northwest corner of the house.

The Nyack of 1820 was an isolated outpost only accessible by dirt roads or the Hudson River. Working with a member of the family that purchased the Tappan patent in 1687, Tunis Smith, Green championed two major transportation and infrastructure projects that literally put Nyack on the map.

Certainly self-interest figured in Green's construction of Nyack's first dock, where Hudson River sloops could deliver lumber for his yard. However, guided by a depth map of the shoreline drafted by Smith, Green inspired a transportation revolution when he helped form the Nyack Steam Boat Association. (A photograph of Tunis's 1825 drawing, possibly the earliest map of Nyack, can be seen at Hannemann's Funeral Home.) Steamboats eventually replaced sloops as the primary mode for passenger and freight transportation until the railroad came to Nyack in 1873.

Nyack in the early 19th century was connected to the world through nature's mighty highway, the Hudson River. But once goods got to our shore, overland transportation was unreliable and arduous. The West Nyack Swamp, which still stymies the efforts of modern engineers, stopped any western progress. There was no way to connect the iron foundry and machine shops of Ramapo to the river.

Once again the tag team of Smith and Green were called upon to apply their talents. Smith surveyed the route and in 1830 Green joined a state commission to oversee construction of the Nyack Turnpike, a road that roughly followed the course of what is now Route 59.

In addition to these important public works, Green was an early trustee of the Nyack Library, a founding member of the Methodist Church, and helped build the Old Stone Meeting House on North Broadway in Upper Nyack. Green died on April 10, 1842, and is buried in Oak Hill Cemetery.

In 2010, Nyack resident John Gromada created a Facebook page dedicated to rallying support to save the Green House. "Saving the building is not an exercise in celebrating the life of one man, but knowing where we came from," says Gromada.

As long as this house stands, we can touch this sandstone and have contact with materials that may have been handled by our ancestors, including anonymous slaves. These stones, quarried from our soil, fueled an economy that was made possible by the bounty of our river, transforming a bunch of homesteads into a community that has survived centuries.

"The Nyack of 1820 was an isolated outpost only accessible by dirt roads or the Hudson."

The John Green House is located at the intersection of Main Street and Gedney in Nyack.

Grace Church

When the founding rector of Grace Episcopal Church, Franklin Babbitt, crossed the Hudson on a sailing sloop from Tarrytown in October 1861, some considered Nyack "an old Dutch place about 50 years behind the times." At age 32, Babbitt swiftly cobbled together a congregation. Two weeks after his arrival at the Burd Street dock, he held his first service and by the end of the month the parish was incorporated.

Babbitt was as much a creative force as a spiritual one during his 56 years as rector. In the early years, he played the role of organist and choirmaster, in addition to his duties as rector and sexton. The greatest legacy to his artistry, however, and the enduring symbol of his organization genius is Grace Church itself.

After building the first Grace Church for $77.49, the congregation outgrew their humble wooden accommodations. As an ardent student of ecclesiastical architecture, Babbitt was determined to construct a church that would rival the finest European sanctuaries. Answering opposition from the more frugal and less aesthetically inclined members of the parish, Babbitt declared, "The very building itself will inspire all whose hearts are open to holy inspiration. It is what a church ought to be."

During the construction phase, several services were held in a roofless sanctuary during storms. There were also memorable debates over everything from brick versus stone to pay-as-you-go versus obtaining a bank loan. Stones and the bank loan prevailed.

It took 14 years of financial struggle before the church was consecrated on May 30, 1882. Those with reservations must have had to concede that Babbitt's vision was divinely inspired. The building functions like a hymn by Handel or a painting by Leonardo da Vinci, transporting those who experience the church to a more ethereal plane.

The current work of the ministry at Grace is as inspirational as the story of the founder and his architectural legacy. There are many wonderful community and cultural programs contained within its stone and stained glass. The music program has four choirs for the flock and produces events and festivals, including the annual Welles Crowther Concert of Remembrance that draws audiences from across the region. The social ministry at Grace provides food and shelter to the homeless through Helping Hands during the winter and the church accommodates 29 different 12-step and recovery programs.

I visited the church for the first time when my niece attended Amazing Grace Circus, a youth art and fitness program, which is also celebrating a significant milestone. The program was created ten years ago during the emotional abyss that followed September 11th. The youth circus has now touched the lives of thousands of students and families through programs in public and private schools and an after school program at Grace.

In the courtyard of Grace Church is a creeping plant that grew from a cutting that Sir Walter Scott gave to Washington Irving, who then gave it to Babbitt. As I recently stood in the garden contemplating the time-traveling vine, I met the church's choirmaster, Robert Burrows, who told me a story worthy of Irving. Apparently, Babbitt laid on his deathbed in the parsonage in a corner room, yards from where we stood, listening to the choir practice his favorite hymn, *I Heard a Voice in Heaven*. Babbitt requested the rehearsal to make sure the choir had mastered his selection for his imminent funeral.

"The building functions like a hymn by Handel or a painting by da Vinci, transporting those who experience the church to a more ethereal plain."

130 1st Ave, Nyack

PILGRIM
BAPTIST CHURCH
FEB 5
MORNING
WORSHIP
SERVICE
10:45 AM
PASTOR

Pilgrim Baptist Church

Pilgrim Baptist Church has found a safe harbor at the corner of High Avenue and North Franklin Street for the last 51 years. The building has multiple slanted roofs and high arched windows that look like the peaks of cresting waves. The pulpit is on the north side of the nave facing south, under a series of massive wooden beams that shelter the pews as the hull does the precious cargo of a sturdy ship. But the pulpit didn't always face south and Pilgrim Baptist Church did not always rest at this spot. The spiritual voyage of this flock began in 1875 above a carriage shop on Burd Street.

Reverend Charles Mayo, Mr. and Mrs. Travis Armstead, and Mrs. Kassie Whines launched the first Pilgrim Baptist Church. When the Armsteads' daughter, Katie, became the congregation's first pianist, the sounds of wagon wheels being repaired and horses being re-shod accompanied her musical selections.

By the time the spirit and size of the faithful outgrew their humble dwelling, the second floor above Spector's Dry Goods store on Main and Bridge Streets was secured. Twenty-eight years of patience and perseverance at this equally modest location were rewarded when a building at 187 Main Street was purchased in 1903 for $1,600, under the leadership of Reverend John Robinson.

Owning their own building must have created a fertile environment for the growth of the congregation. In 1938, a mortgage-burning banquet was presided over by Reverend W.C. Taylor. By 1955, before the parishioners could get comfortable, the Pilgrim family required a larger house of worship and the search began again.

On May 1, 1961, the Most Worshipful Prince Hall Grand Lodge of the State of New York laid a cornerstone for the congregation at the new location on North Franklin Street. The dwindling attendance of a German Presbyterian parish provided Pilgrim with this new sanctuary. The chapel on Main Street was sold to Hollingswood Memorial Temple for $5,000.

After decades of temporary accommodations and transitions, Pilgrim had found a permanent home. A program of reconstruction and renovation was undertaken to make sure that spatial limitations would not necessitate another move. Some of those changes included changing the orientation of the pulpit from east to south and moving the entrance from Franklin Street to High Avenue. In 1994, the church observed another mortgage-burning celebration. The sojourn was finally over, Pilgrim had its home.

A period of tranquility was further cemented by the arrival of a new pastor in 1990. Reverend Dr. Willie L. Hairston first stepped into the pulpit at Pilgrim as a guest preacher from Mount Nebo Baptist Church in the Bronx, New York. When the pulpit was later declared vacant, the membership of Pilgrim voted to make Reverend Hairston their leader. His tenure has brought both dynamic programming and institutional stability to Pilgrim.

African American churches have anchored a community that has been buffeted by unpredictable and unforgiving political and economic forces. Even when this congregation lacked a formal tabernacle, they continued to serve as an additional safe haven for generations of African American families in Nyack.

"African American churches have anchored a community that has been buffeted by unpredictable and unforgiving political and economic forces."

Pilgrim Baptist Church is located at the corner of High Avenue and North Franklin Street in Nyack.

NYACK PUBLIC LIBRARY
BOOK RETURN
BATSON 2012

The Nyack Library

More than 200 years ago, *Nicholas Green* and Tunis Depew sowed the seeds that would become the Nyack Library. A membership fee of $90 a year was required to join the "first edition" of our community's book depository. Their institution was undoubtedly modeled on Benjamin Franklin's Library Company of Philadelphia, considered to be the first lending library in North America.

In 1872, the Reverend Stephen Merritt Jr. established the next incarnation of a library in Nyack as part of the Young Men's Christian Association, during a period when the village was emerging as a regional capitol. Factories, steamboats, and the Nyack Turnpike helped grow the village to 3,500 people. The swelling population brought new problems. Nyack's streets were crowded with "tobacco-chewing street loafers" according to a letter to the editor in the *Rockland County Journal.*

The newly-incorporated village administration must have been pleased to see a private effort to promote literacy and self-improvement. As a Methodist minister, Merritt imbued the YMCA with the tenets of the Temperance Movement. In 1873, the collection included 200 volumes that advocated abstinence from alcohol.

Nyack's YMCA, two banks, and many businesses may have succumbed to the economic depression of 1878, but Merritt's collection of books endured. The existing collection was subsequently reorganized into the nucleus of a resurgent public library. By-laws were adopted and in January 1879 the Nyack Library was reborn.

Local stationer and news dealer John Haeselbarth served as librarian and his store on Main Street and Broadway became the reading room. On September 10, 1890, the trustees took steps to create a proper library setting, where readers did not have to compete with shoppers for the librarian's attention. Rooms were rented on DePew Avenue for $275 per year and Emma Thornburn, who previously served as the YMCA's librarian, was returned to her post.

There was still one big transformation ahead for our library, the journey from fee to free. According to the founding documents, "any person might become a member by payment of $1." An additional dollar would have to be paid annually for the right to borrow books. In February 1893 yearly charges were dropped, making the library truly public.

In 1903, Andrew Carnegie was supporting the construction of libraries across America. Communities across the country competed for a contribution from Carnegie and his funding did not come without strings.

Local governments needed to agree to allocate annually 10% of Carnegie's donation to maintain the library he would build. If his terms were met, Carnegie would pledge $2 per resident. The population of the three river villages—Nyack, Upper Nyack, South Nyack—was 7,500 at the end of the 19th century. The three village boards voted to increase library funding from $1,200 per year to $1,500, or 10% of Carnegie's eventual $15,000 gift. Nyack's Library was one of 1,689 public libraries Andrew Carnegie supported in 1,419 communities across America.

The building was designed by acclaimed local architects the Emery Brothers and Mr. J. B. Simonson. A spacious annex of metal and glass, designed by architect, Michael Esmay, was completed in 2011.

The ten-ton rock standing outside the library is dedicated to Abraham Lincoln and the Union Army. On June 13, 1908, it was dragged from the banks of the Hudson River by a team of 18 horses and 100 men.

"Nyack's Library was one of 1,689 Andrew Carnegie supported in 1,419 communities across America."

Nyack Library is located at 59 South Broadway, Nyack.

MUSIC
in the garden
Hopper House
THURSDAY
NIGHT
CONCERTS
7:30 P.M
BATSON 8.4.12

Hopper House

The childhood home of one of America's greatest visual artists, Edward Hopper, was saved from destruction in the early 1970s by an ad-hoc coalition that included neighbors, Rotarians, labor unions, students, and artists. Not many causes can assemble the vast cross-section of humanity and contributions that were necessary to save a building that was literally a few signatures away from condemnation. Hopper's iconic and evocative paintings linger on man-made landscapes, both urban and semi-rural. In Hopper's world, the landscape shares equal billing with the human figure. Often the setting is the leading lady. The preservation of Hopper's house allows us to view the artist in relation to his aboriginal setting. Thanks to a local tradition of historic preservation and the absence of over-development, the majority of the village that you see today is very close in scale and population density that was Nyack in the early 20th century, when Hopper was a child.

A short walk from this house to the north will bring you to the First Baptist Church, a sanctuary that was founded in 1851 by Hopper's great-grandfather. The enterprise that generated the income that allowed Hopper to pursue a career in the arts was G. H. Hopper's Dry Goods Store, operated by his father from a storefront that is now Grace's Thrift Shop several blocks south of the family home.

In 1979, former Hopper House Board Chair, Alan Gussow, wrote "half of all the business blocks standing in Nyack in 1950 were built in the 1880s and 1890s" during Hopper's childhood. These brownstone brick facades, when bathed in the light reflected off the Hudson, produced the saturated tones that form the color palate in many of Hopper's most important paintings, such as *Early Sunday Morning* (1930).

Hopper left home after graduating from Nyack High School, but would return to visit his sister, Marion, who lived in the house until her death in 1965. The artist died on May 15, 1967, and his wife of over 40 years, artist Josephine Verstille Nivison, passed away a year later. The demise of this entire cohort of the Hopper family over such a short span put the future of the family home in jeopardy. After Marion's death, the house became an abandoned eyesore inhabited by squatters.

When Jeffrey and Barbara Arnold intervened to save the house of their late neighbor Marion in 1970, a real estate investor with plans to demolish the home and build apartments had already purchased the property from the Hopper Estate. The Arnolds were able to raise $15,000 from gifts and interest-free loans from concerned citizens to buy back Hopper's house.

This was the beginning of what local architect and historian, Win Perry, calls the greatest and most exciting adventure of his life. Perry volunteered to coordinate the restoration project. The steady stream of people who answered the call to save Hopper's house must have resembled an Amish barn raising.

Thanks to decades of volunteer labor from board members and supporters, the property is now listed on the National Registry of Historic Places and functions as the Edward Hopper House Art Center, a climate-controlled gallery space with a packed schedule of world-class exhibitions, performances, and screenings.

Edward Hopper celebrated the essence of his hometown on canvas, making Nyack recognizable to art lovers everywhere. If these volunteers had not returned the favor, we would not benefit from the cultural pilgrims from around the world who come to this village to see what inspired Edward Hopper.

"Edward Hopper celebrated the essence of his hometown on canvas, making Nyack recognizable to art lovers everywhere."

Hopper House is located at 82 North Broadway, Nyack. edwardhopperhouse.org

BATSON 8-11-12

AUGUST 14, 2012

Hopper Happens

In 2004, Hopper was happening globally in London when 420,000 people visited the Edward Hopper exhibit at the Tate Gallery in only three months. In 2006, Hopper happened for comedian Steve Martin who sold Hopper's painting *Hotel Window* (1955) for $26 million at a Sotheby's auction. Locally, *Hopper Happens* whenever you drive past the Northwest corner of North Broadway and School Street in Upper Nyack and see the empty storefront that was the inspiration for Hopper's 1948 painting, *Seven A.M.*, and this week's sketch.

During the summer of 2011, this village celebrated the 40th anniversary of the restoration and transformation of the painter's boyhood home into the Edward Hopper House Art Center. In addition to the Hopper paintings on loan from the Whitney Museum of American Art shown inside, multimedia artist and Nyack resident Kris Burns helped take Hopper to the streets of the village though her summer long festival, *Hopper Happens.* The celebration of Hopper's life and work included flash mobs, site-specific slide projections, and the showing of Hopper inspired movies.

"I got caught in the whirlwind of Kris Burns's flash mobs and projections in 2011 at the first Hopper Happens festival."

In 2012, Burns did it again, with more films and new media innovations. Some elements were hidden in plain sight around the village, which required that you pass your digital device over a QR code decal to view.

Burns is well-positioned to promote Hopper's contributions to our culture as an artist-in-residence at the Edward Hopper House Art Center. Her workspace is situated in one of Hopper's childhood bedrooms. Burns has organized numerous cultural and community programs in Nyack, including co-founding Rivertown Film and producing a few seasons of *Mostly Music.* In 2010, she received the County Executive Arts Award for Supporter of the Arts.

I got caught in the whirlwind of Burns's public art activity in 2011 at the first *Hopper Happens* festival. One evening I witnessed a roaming flash mob of people dressed in period clothing striking Hopperesque poses. A week later, I viewed the paintings of Hopper and artists inspired by our native son projected on a wall. A month later, in homage to both Hopper and Burns, and their potent muse, the Village of Nyack, I started this sketch log.

This sketch log honors Hopper's *Seven A.M.*. I visited the Upper Nyack corner that Hopper captured on canvas, arriving at the scene at the exact time that the title of the painting suggests. At that hour of the day, the color of the light is the main character. The simple plot of a rising sun illuminating the natural and man-made landscape is universal and timeless.

The continuation of these outdoor, interactive tributes can help secure Nyack as an important destination for worldwide Hopper fans. If we are interested in encouraging part of the massive audience that visited the Tate Gallery in London for the 2004 exhibit to make a pilgrimage to Nyack, we need to ensure that *Hopper Happens* again and again and again.

BASON
2014

JULY 10, 2014

Hip Hopper Hooray!

Edward Hopper's posthumous popularity continues to soar. In April 2014, *Art Everywhere U.S.* conducted a poll to see what paintings Americans wanted displayed nationally on billboards, bus shelters, and subway platforms. *Nighthawks* (1942) by Edward Hopper received the most votes.

With Hopper's childhood home converted to an arts center on North Broadway in Nyack, and his final resting place around the corner at Oak Hill Cemetery, it's time to roll out the welcome mat for the world to visit the village that nurtured the talent of our country's favorite visual artist.

Other municipalities are seeking to mine the gold that is in the pigment of Hopper's paintings. "Chicago is a world-class city with phenomenal cultural institutions that house iconic works of art," stated Chicago Mayor Rahm Emanuel. "I am proud that the Art Institute of Chicago . . . is providing 12 paintings to the Art Everywhere outdoor exhibit from its renowned collection, including the most popular painting Nighthawks." If the mayor of the nation's third largest city is dropping Edward Hopper's name to attract tourists, maybe Nyack should stake a larger claim to our hometown hero.

As interest in the artist grows, Nyack has the back story to meet the unquenchable thirst for Hopper. International art pilgrims make up an increasing segment of visitors to the Edward Hopper House Art Center at 82 North Broadway, according to Hopper House Director, Victoria Hertz. "I would say 75% of our daily visitors are from outside Rockland and half of those are from outside the United States. Just last week we had visitors from Germany and Australia," Hertz stated.

Born in Nyack in 1882, Hopper graduated from Liberty School when it was kindergarten through 12th grade. He lived here into the 1920s, but would return to visit his sister, Marion, who occupied the house he grew up in until her death in 1965. The artist died on May 15, 1967, and his wife of over 40 years, artist Josephine Verstille Nivison, passed away a year later.

There are two measures of status in the art world—the price artists' paintings fetch at auction and attendance at major exhibitions. In both arenas, Edward Hopper is an enduring heavy weight cultural champion.

December 2013: *East Wind Over Weehawken* (1934) sold for $40.5 million at Christie's sale of American art.

2006: Comedian Steve Martin sold Hopper's painting *Hotel Window* (1955) for $26 million at a Sotheby's auction.

2004: The Edward Hopper exhibit at the Tate Gallery in London, England, was visited by 420,000 people in only three months.

Summer 2012: Middlebury College received 10,000 visitors to their Hopper exhibit. The population of Middlebury, Vermont is 8,000.

October 2012-February 2013: Hopper's retrospective at the Grand Palais in Paris was viewed by 780,000 people. The exhibit was so popular that for the last few days the museum stayed open around the clock.

Many towns have scenic views of the Hudson River, are conveniently located to transportation routes, and have quaint downtowns that tempt travelers and tourists alike to stop to spend some time and money. But only Nyack has Edward Hopper.

"In April 2014, Americans voted "Nighthawks" by Edward Hopper as the painting they would most like to see displayed nationally on billboards, bus shelters, and subway platforms."

FEBRUARY 7, 2012

Hopper Meets Hitchcock

The building in Haverstraw that is the subject of Edward Hopper's 1925 painting, *House by the Railroad*, still proudly stands. The haunting depiction of the three-story house came to the attention of the cast and crew of Alfred Hitchcock's movie classic, *Psycho*. Hopper's painting inspired not only the design of the Bates Mansion in the 1960 production, but the mood of the film as well.

"Hopper's painting of a house in Haverstraw inspired the design of the Bates Mansion in the 1960 Hitchcock classic, Psycho, and the mood of the film as well."

House by the Railroad depicts an exquisite Victorian-style home, located on Route 9W just south of St. Peter's Cemetery. His composition shows a solitary structure, cut off from the world by a system of railroad tracks like those rapidly dissecting American communities during the mid-20th century.

Today, the building is still visually incarcerated by a heavily trafficked road, power lines, chain-link fencing, and the railroad that gave the original painting its name and theme. In Hitchcock's film, a newly constructed interstate highway isolates the Bates motel and mansion, stranding Tony Perkins's character to stew in his psychosis.

Before the industrialization of transportation by steam and fossil fuel-powered vehicles, every town in America was a stop along the route to any nearby destination. After these innovations, the location of railroad lines and highways determined economic winners and losers. If you didn't have a depot or an off ramp, you were left behind by those seeking more convenient modes of transportation. Hopper's painting and Hitchcock's film portray the abrupt transitions that swept communities of stately manors into the trash heap of history.

In 1919, Rockland County Attorney General, Thomas Gagan, bought the house. His daughter, Amo, lived there for 50 years. According to legend, as a 13-year- old, she saw Hopper seated at his portable easel on the gravel sidings of the train track creating the painting that would become a masterpiece of American art and the prototype for an iconic image from American cinema. I chose the same perspective for my sketch.

The current owners have restored the exterior of the house to a pristine state that would have pleased Hopper and Hitchcock. The lawn is manicured, the original clapboard and windows have been expertly restored. With its widow's peak, curved mansard roof, and shut blinds, I thought I had stumbled upon an architectural time capsule. The building came to life as the door swung open and I met the owner, Lori.

Lori and her husband, Edwin, are the loving stewards of this American treasure. Edwin didn't know the Hopper-Hitchcock connection when he acquired the property. He soon noticed that cars would pull into his driveway to marvel in silence or snap photos of his house. Now, reproductions of the Hopper painting, as well as renditions by friends and relatives, adorn the interior of the house (except in rooms formed by the hourglass-shaped roof with sloping walls that cannot accommodate hanging pictures).

Thanks to the efforts of the Edward Hopper House Art Center, one of our greatest assets, the legacy of Edward Hopper remains relevant. It would be the sweetest irony that the man who feared that small town America was dying was the impetus for the revival of the village of his birth.

1889
JOSEP

House Haunted by Art

When printmaker Sylvia Roth moved into her home in South Nyack in 1977, she had no idea it was the birthplace of a major figure in American art, Joseph Cornell. This house on Piermont Avenue seems to have had its own designs on selecting artistic occupants for over a century.

Emily Dickinson, Cornell's enduring muse, wrote that "nature is a haunted house, but art is a house that tries to be haunted." As Roth describes the creative output of subsequent generations of her family, one begins to suspect that this is a house haunted by art.

This house on Piermont Avenue was the childhood home of Joseph Cornell. His father, Joseph, was a well-to-do designer and his mother, Helen Ten Broeck Storms Cornell, was a kindergarten teacher. He had two sisters, Elizabeth and Helen, and one brother, Robert.

When his father died in 1917, Cornell's family moved to Queens, N.Y. He lived for most of his life in a small, wooden-frame house on Utopia Parkway with his mother and his brother, Robert. Cornell devoted much of his life to the care of his brother, who had cerebral palsy. Cornell became a recluse and other than a few years at the Philips Academy in Andover, Massachusetts, he never left the metropolitan New York City area. His art work, however, became internationally recognized, collected, and exhibited.

According to the artist and writer, Lee Mamunes, a docent at the Edward Hopper House Art Center, "Cornell was a true eccentric and completely self-taught. He was not a sculptor or painter. He was a collector. In his late 20s, he began to assemble fragments of everyday life, including memories of his happy childhood in Nyack, placing them in glass-fronted shadow boxes resembling tiny stage sets."

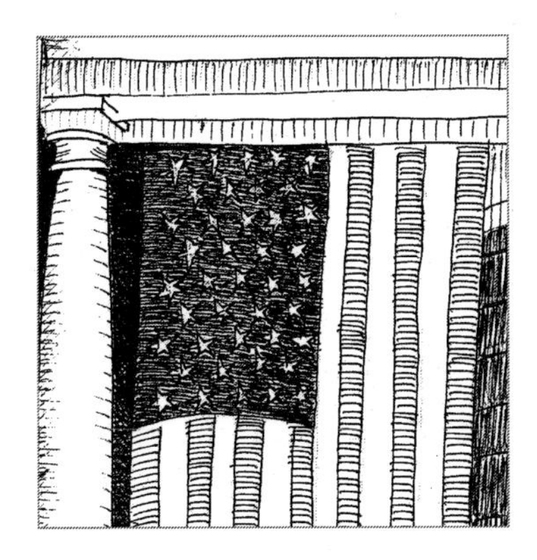

"This house on Piermont Avenue seems to have its own designs, selecting artistic occupants for over a century including Joseph Cornell, Ralph Pearson, John Beerman and Sylvia Roth."

I understand there are many artists in your family.

For many, many years I was a printmaker. I had my own studio, *Hudson River Editions.* I was making my own art, etchings and paintings, ever since I was ten.

My mother, Faye, painted. As an immigrant, she never had a chance to get an art education. But she loved to paint flowers and birds. My daughter Susie is a therapist and bereavement counselor at United Hospice of Rockland and she also has a private practice. And she still makes art. Susan's twin, Anna Hays, is a writer and my son, SJ, is a screenwriter. Susie met her ex-husband, John Beerman, at Skowhegan, an artists' colony in Maine. He is a well-known landscape artist. My granddaughter, Hannah Faye, is at Bard College. She is going to make painting her life. Susie's son, Joey, is a musician and plays bass at the conservatory at SUNY Purchase.

Now tell me about the second creative occupant you discovered.

A woman was in town for her Nyack High School reunion and wanted to visit the home where she grew up. Her father, Ralph Pearson, was a well-known printmaker who wrote the book *How to Look at Modern Pictures.* As we walked with her through the house, she pointed at one room as the place where he did his printmaking. I had just had the floor in that very room reinforced to install a 2,000 pound etching press.

Rockland Center for the Arts

In the contest to draw an audience for the arts, Rockland County is David to the Goliath of New York City. But when it comes to attracting artists to take up residence, the region has assembled a pantheon of American cultural deities worthy of Mount Olympus. Figures like actor Helen Hayes, composer Aaron Copland, painter Edward Hopper, and writer Ben Hecht, to name a few, made their homes in our neck of the woods. Fortunately for us, a few of these important creative artists combined their efforts to leave us a living institutional legacy: The Rockland Center for the Arts.

Helen Hayes christened the enduring voyage of this creative arts organization in 1949. She staged a benefit performance of *The Glass Menagerie* at Nyack High School. The play's author, Tennessee Williams, drove from Manhattan to attend the performance. On his way, he picked up his friend, author and South Nyack resident, Carson McCullers. Joining Hayes on stage was the young actress, Julie Harris.

The performance funded the work of the Rockland Foundation; the organization would change its name to Rockland Center for the Arts or RoCA in 1970. Hayes was joined in this effort of cultural institution building by some of the most celebrated names in the arts, including Copland, Paulette Goddard, Kurt Weill, Maxwell Anderson, and Lotte Lenya. Mary Mowbray-Clarke, who, with husband John Fredrick and abstract artist Arthur B. Davies, organized the 1913 *Armory Show* in New York City that introduced French Impressionism and launched the modern art movement in America (including the work of Edward Hopper). RoCA described their mission in a 1946 essay: "To share with their neighbors whatever insights and power of expression they possess, to help in the quickening of talent among children, to take advantage of the presence in Rockland County of so many creative people."

For its first few years, the organization operated from the basement of a building at 35 North Broadway. The group found a permanent home in 1949 when Anne Emerson bequeathed her property in West Nyack to RoCA. The parcel included a stone and clapboard house dating from the late 1800s, a small barn, and a chicken coop situated on ten acres.

In 1970, Helen Hayes headlined a fundraiser at the dedication of a new building for RoCA designed by local architect, Charles Winter, to accommodate galleries, studios, and offices. The sprawling grounds have been transformed into the Catherine Konner Sculpture Park, which currently features 14 pieces of outdoor and site-specific sculpture.

Under the direction of an active board and the guidance of Executive Director Julianne Ramos, RoCA has stayed true to the vision Mowbray-Clarke articulated in 1946. RoCA employs 45 instructors who offer 200 arts classes annually for everyone from the advanced practitioner to the hobbyist. For 53 summers, RoCA has offered a day camp-style arts program for children ages 5 to 12.

Artistic Director, Lynn Stein, coordinates programs at RoCA. As a visual and performing artist (she paints and is a jazz vocalist), Stein personifies the multidisciplinary sensibilities that RoCA's founders embraced.

The face that frames the building in my sketch is part of an installation titled, "Red Faces," by Monica Banks. This work was part of a series of dozens of faces exhibited in Times Square from 1996 until 2009. Like many of the sculptures that are on display in the Catherine Konner Sculpture Park, the Banks installation was made possible with the cooperation of New York City's Public Art Fund.

"When it comes to attracting artists to take up residence, the region has assembled a pantheon of American cultural deities worthy of Mount Olympus."

RoCA is located at 27 Greenbush Road, West Nyack. rocklandartcenter.org

DECEMBER 4, 2012

Helen Hayes MacArthur

Legend has it that when Helen Hayes MacArthur first saw this fine example of Italianate architecture on North Broadway, her husband, playwright Charles MacArthur, told her it would cost them a "pretty penny." As a name, it stuck. From 1934 to 1990, the actress known to the world as the First Lady of American Theater lived here in the Village of Nyack as a mother, wife, book lover, neighbor, and civic leader, not as a celebrity.

Following are Mrs. MacArthur's reflections on her experiences in Nyack. A transcript of a speech where much of this text was taken, along with other extraordinary documents and artifacts, can be found in the Local History Room of the Nyack Library.

"When Helen Hayes MacArthur first saw this fine example of Italianate architecture on North Broadway, her husband, playwright Charles MacArthur told her it would cost them a pretty penny."

Our Courting Days

During our courting days, Charlie liked to bring me, on a Sunday afternoon, to Tarrytown by train and then by the little snub-nosed ferry to Nyack, a good half hour's river trip, complete with Italian serenaders, accordion, violin, and tenor. Just right for lovers.

On our first visit, we went directly to the frame house on South Boulevard which had been the last home of the MacArthurs as a family. It was near the Missionary Institute where the Rev. William T. MacArthur had been a preacher in residence and a mighty stirring one from all accounts.

Starting a Trend

We brought friends who would have us clinging with them to Long Island. We lured them with picnics by the river. Once they saw our future estate, they were invariably filled with wonder and envy.

Ben Hecht bought a house for himself on Perry Lane, Joshua and Nedda Logan came seriously house-hunting. We looked to have started a trend.

Forces of Magic

As we passed along South Boulevard, our progress was slowed to a crawl by four elephants, shuffling down the center, tail in trunk. They seemed to be alone and they seemed to know where they were going and seemed bored. That was the first inkling we had that this was no ordinary, old-fashioned, small river town.

Oom, the Omnipotent

That is how we became acquainted with Dr. Bernard, ex-barber from Brooklyn, and then Oom, the Omnipotent, the yoga big-wig. His Clarkstown Country Club was a huge compound, teaming with seekers after health and spiritual awareness. There was also a good sized menagerie.

When the Officers Arrived at Poolside

There was a night when a neighbor, who had never relaxed her vigilance on behalf of the community's propriety, registered a complaint to the Nyack Police. When the officers arrived at poolside, they were greeted by the bride-to-be, Bobby Boll, and the Bridegroom-to-be, Lew Herndon, and the wedding party, made up mostly of Nyack's old families. Red-faced, the police retired with the admonition, "Keep it down Bobby." Poor dears, those cops had missed out on a night when Katherine Hepburn, in bra and shorts, had given a superb exhibition of diving in the pool.

Today's sketch is not from life, or a photo, but from Edward Hopper's 1939 painting of *Pretty Penny*. Hopper was reluctant to accept the commission, considering the assignment "tradesman's," as opposed to "fine art" work. The painting that Hopper produced is almost light hearted, a radical departure from most of his canvases.

PLAYHOUSE
The Tappan Zee PLAYHOUSE
KING DONOVAN
BELLS ARE RINGING
IMOGENE COCA

SEPTEMBER 24, 2013

Tappan Zee Playhouse

The parcel at the corner of Church Street and South Broadway has a development cycle similar to the cicada. The 17-year siesta of those insects who returned to Nyack in the spring of 2013 is actually shorter than the period of hibernation between transitions at this once famous facade. Occupants and sometimes buildings come and go with two or three decades-long lulls before the next incarnation.

"The Tappan Zee Playhouse was a major stop in the summer stock circuit, drawing the greatest performing artists in the world."

The land was first developed by Aaron L. Christie as a carriage factory in 1835. It later became a blacksmith's shop and stable and then a grocery, butcher, and candy store.

James Kilby was first in the line of impresarios to bring theater to Broadway in Nyack. In 1907, Kilby razed the building with the intent to build a performance space. The time period between the demolition and construction was so long, however, that the excavated foundation became known as Kilby's Folly.

The project finally came to fruition in 1911 when prominent jurist Arthur S. Tompkins signed on as a partner. The Broadway Theater became a stage for vaudeville and photoplays, the silent films of the time, with a sound track supplied by a full orchestra. They enjoyed packed houses until competition from The Rockland Theater on North Broadway and the depression ended their run.

The next period of dormancy, from 1931 until 1957, was about a decade longer than the cicada's nap. But this time, the theater that Bruce Becker and Honey Waldman roused from its slumber as the Tappan Zee Playhouse was an instant hit.

The Tappan Zee Playhouse was a major stop in the summer stock circuit, drawing the greatest performing artists in the world to take the stage and, occasionally, to fill the plush velvet seats. In 1964, Jan Degenshein, an award-winning local architect and planner, saw Eliot Gould and a young ingénue, Liza Minnelli in *The Fantasticks,* "That would be the stuff of legend right there," he recalled, "but in the box next to me I saw Gould's new bride, Barbara Streisand."

A fire in 1976 darkened the stage and led to the next interregnum. A succession of initiatives from residents and village government were undertaken to keep the Tappan Zee Playhouse a functioning theater. Toward that end, the building was placed on the national register of historic places (it was subsequently de-registered) and purchased by the village to prevent the building from being developed by a party not interested in the historic and cultural significance of the property.

The playhouse was renamed for Helen Hayes, the beloved Nyack resident known as the First Lady of the American Theater, as an attempt to rally support. Momentum did not shift, controversies ensued, and the Hayes name and dreams for preserving the legacy of the playhouse were redirected to the Nyack Cinema on Main Street. Those hopes and the next iteration of the venue, called Riverspace, were literally and figuratively drowned by flood waters and bogged down by subsequent legal entanglements.

But the structure that has supplied Nyack with carriages, meat, candy, burlesque, silent movies, and a steady stream of celebrities will rise again, cicada-like.

Main Stage

Elmwood Playhouse

The history of the Elmwood Playhouse is so extensive they have their own historian. Mike Gnazzo holds that job, and a slew of others. In his primary role as Lighting Designer, Gnazzo animates and enhances the action on the stage. As historian, he sheds light on the activities of a volunteer theater company that has been staging plays in Nyack since 1947. For their first ten years, the company was itinerant, performing in homes, schools, hotels, and a short run at the Rockland Psychiatric Hospital. The troupe had as many names in the early years as venues, performing as the Curtain Callers, the Camp Shanks Players, and the Rockland Community Theater. It didn't matter what they were called or where they performed, according to Gnazzo, "they were a group of people who wanted to get together and stage plays."

In 1957, the company found a permanent home and a lasting name. Funds were raised to purchase St. Paul's Lutheran Church on Park Street, which was constructed in 1898, for $8,000. For their inaugural performance of *Bus Stop*, the audience sat on church pews. The troupe borrowed their name from the first word of the phrase that was used to remind residents of their phone number prefix: *Elmwood 8.*

"Elmwood Playhouse is approaching their 350th production with an estimated audience over the last 66 seasons surpassing 300,000."

Under the leadership of Board Chair Elaine Vogel, they acquired the adjoining properties on New Street that included a hair salon, a taxi stand, and a furniture warehouse. The annex now houses the theater's scenic workshop, storage spaces for lighting, props and costumes, dressing rooms, and rehearsal studios that are connected by a series of mazelike passages.

Over the years, many individuals have made memorable contributions to the company. Bob Olson designed 216 shows before his untimely death in 2009. Not only did he enrich the lives of Nyack residents directly through his craft, he launched the careers of two women who have succeeded on theater's greatest stages, entertaining millions.

Peggy Eisenhauer, nicknamed "Girlie" by Olson when she was 13, went on to win a Tony for her lighting design for *Bring In Da Noise, Bring In Da Funk.* Jennie Marino has created specialty props for *Phantom of the Opera* and *Les Misérables.* Olson dubbed Marino, who is still active with the company, "the powerful Katrinka."

Many of the Life Members of the troupe have over 30 years of service. It is also common to see several members of families working together. Jennie Marino's son, Matthew, worked on the lighting for the next Elmwood play, *Living Out,* a production that is being directed by Mike Gnazzo's wife, Kathy. The current Board Chairman and frequent performer, Larry Beckerle, was brought onto the stage by his mother Denise. There is something devout in the length and intensity of the volunteer commitment of the Elmwood Playhouse members. Could it be that this building, with its ecclesiastic peak and catacombs full of props and costumes has become a cathedral for musicals, comedy, and drama?

The company is approaching its 350th production and Mike Gnazzo estimates that the audience over the last 66 seasons surpasses 300,000. Driven by the devotion of 1,570 people who have stood on the stage of this intimate 99-seat theater and the 216 people who have served on the Board, the Elmwood Playhouse has kept a sacred theatrical oath. Where larger, commercial ventures have come and gone, this humble collective of true believers makes sure that in Nyack the show goes on.

10 Park Street, Nyack
elmwoodplayhouse.com

NYACK VILLAGE
THEATRE
F.W.

APRIL 17, 2012

Nyack Village Theatre

The Nyack Village Theatre sign is unassuming and you might just walk on by, but that would be a mistake. One exposure to the live content that is produced from this 49-seat black box theater space will stop you in your tracks. Nestled one story above the site that was once F.W. Woolworth is an expanding multimedia arts organization founded by 1980's rocker-turned-impresario, Richard Quinn.

The arts center appeared on my radar screen last Halloween, when I saw a poster advertising a midnight showing of *The Rocky Horror Picture Show*. As a teenager, I saw the cult classic more times than I care to admit across the street when what is now Riverspace was a garden-variety movie theater.

When *Rocky Horror* exploded onto the counter-cultural consciousness of America in 1975, Quinn was a recent high school grad getting his real education in legendary New York City clubs like Max's Kansas City and CBGB's. This was the moment when acts like Talking Heads, Lou Reed, Patti Smith, The Ramones, and Blondie were emerging on the music scene. His band, Quinn and the Eskimos, would later play those same venues.

The Nyack Village Theatre that Quinn opened in 2006 is influenced by the energy and eclecticism of the New York art scene of the early 1980s. It was in the economically ravaged East Village that Punk, New Wave, Hip Hop, and graffiti cultures converged in downtown nightclubs and art galleries. "I like to think of myself in the tradition of Andy Warhol. I'm building an art factory," said Quinn of one of the sources of his inspiration. If the Nyack Village Theatre is a factory, there are several divisions that manufacture a variety of art products. The theater is actually a spin-off of two other endeavors.

In 2003, Quinn launched Rockland World Radio, an online broadcast station that's streams live video of all programming. Modern Metro Zine, or MMZ, offers the insight and expertise of the hosts of the Internet program in print form.

The media platform that Quinn has built is like a dim sum menu of all that was excellent about New York City in the late 20th century. It's a mash up of several pioneering cultural institutions combining the political edge of WBAI, the bold experimentalism of Joseph Papp's Public Theater, the bombast of CBGB's, and the intimate, sloped screening-room vibe of the Thalia.

The Nyack Village Theatre is a place where Quinn told me he hoped to introduce the public to art, performance, and information that they can't find anywhere else. When I challenged him to name something that fit that bill he described the screening of never before seen footage from an unreleased documentary about Jimi Hendrix by Dave Kramer. The film was accompanied by a showing of original artwork created by Jimi Hendrix and owned by the family of drummer Christian Van den Hueval.

On a recent Sunday, Quinn showed a free matinee exhibition of *Fresh, the Movie*. The filmmakers decry the collapse of the symbiotic cycle between animals and plants that has resulted from the advent of corporate agriculture that jeopardizes our health and our food supply.

Quinn feels that there is a similar life cycle between the artist and the audience. "The artist needs the audience to exist and the audience needs art to survive. Art is nourishment for the soul," said Quinn. So if you are hungry for some art, Quinn serves it up online, in print, and on stage.

"The Nyack Village Theatre that Quinn opened in 2006 is influenced by the energy and eclecticism of the New York art scene of the early 1980s."

94 Main Street, Nyack
nyackvillagetheatre.com

MAY 7, 2013

The Trip to Bountiful

Nyack was a stop on *The Trip to Bountiful*. The play of that name was just nominated for a Tony Award for best revival, and its author, Horton Foote, lived in this house in Upper Nyack in the 1950s. Foote joined theater greats Helen Hayes, Charles MacArthur, Ben Hecht, and Carson McCullers, who called our village home. For a moment in time, if you wanted to find some of the most important figures in American theater, you need only take a stroll down Broadway—in Nyack.

"For a moment in time, if you wanted to find some of the most important figures in American theater, you need only take a stroll down Broadway – in Nyack."

Foote moved to Nyack from New York City with his wife, Lillian, and three children. His fourth child was born at Nyack Hospital. When Foote arrived, he was already a prolific and successful playwright and a major force in the new media of the day, television.

The Trip to Bountiful originally aired on NBC on March 1, 1953. Lillian Gish and Eva Marie Saint reprised their roles on Broadway a year later at what was then Henry Miller's Theater. The recent revival of that play, directed by Michael Wilson, opened 60 years later at the same venue, which has been extensively renovated and is now named for Stephen Sondheim.

Nyack resident and composer, John Gromada, who was nominated for Best Sound Design for the revival of *Bountiful*, first worked with Horton Foote on the 2000 production of *The Carpetbaggers Children* with Jean Stapleton at Lincoln Center Theater. Although Foote no longer lived in Nyack when they met, Gromada said that he and the playwright bonded over their mutual affection for our river village. Over the years, Gromada has worked on six Horton Foote projects.

Hallie Foote was six when the family arrived in Nyack. She remembers her transplanted city cat eating the heads off all of her mother's tulips at their first home on North Broadway and family picnics on the banks of the Hudson River.

Several years after moving to Nyack, Foote crafted a script that not only won him an Academy Award, but also helped create a national discussion about racial injustice. That screenplay, *To Kill a Mockingbird*, was written at the family's second Nyack home.

Hallie describes a procession of creative heavyweights visiting their house on Ferris Lane in South Nyack. "Alan Pakula, who went on to direct *All the President's Men*, was the producer for *To Kill a Mockingbird* and spent a lot of time meeting with my father. Bob Mulligan, the director, was there and I believe that Harper Lee came once." Lee wrote the best-selling book that inspired the film.

Soon after winning the Academy Award for the script, Foote relocated his family to New Hampshire. The artistic and creative demands of the Horton Foote estate now fall on Hallie's shoulders. She recently formed the Horton Foote Legacy Foundation to promote her father's work as well as his craft. "We provide access to my father's childhood home in Wharton, Texas, as a residence for writers." A great deal of the content of Foote's work, including the *Orphan's Home Cycle* and *The Trip to Bountiful*, is drawn from that region.

An accomplished actor, Hallie starred in *Dividing the Estate*, in 2008, and *The Old Friends*, in 2013. Along with director Michael Wilson, composer John Gromada, and her husband, actor Devon Abner, she has created an ensemble that is interpreting the work of Horton Foote for new and expanding audiences.

BASON 9.10.12

Carson McCullers

Carson McCullers came to Nyack in 1945 to convalesce and create. For 22 years she found a place to do both, completing *The Member of the Wedding*, *The Ballad of the Sad Café*, and *Clock Without Hands*. McCullers moved to the village five years after the publication of her acclaimed first novel, *The Heart is a Lonely Hunter.* On September 29, 1967, her heart and vascular system, weakened by a litany of ailments and the strain from the kind of despondency that often afflicts great artists, finally surrendered.

The years that McCullers lived a few steps from downtown Nyack were divided between periods of productivity and infirmity. In his foreword to Virginia Spencer Carr's definitive biography of the author, playwright Tennessee Williams wrote, "I hope that with increasing study of Carson McCullers it will be recognized, generally, that despite the early onset of her many illnesses, she was, in her spirit, a person of rare and luminous health."

Ironically, it was the early onset of illness that both shortened her life and led her to literature. She first considered becoming a writer during a bout of pneumonia, her first serious health scare, when she was 15 years old. McCullers identified with Eugene O'Neill, an author who was himself inspired to become a playwright during his recovery from tuberculosis. Her frail health deprived McCullers of the stamina required to pursue her dream of becoming a concert pianist. In 1936, during another doctor-ordered respite in her hometown of Columbus, Georgia, she pieced together the characters and circumstances that would become *The Heart is a Lonely Hunter.*

Richard Wright, author of *Native Son*, was deeply moved by the transcendent quality of McCullers's prose. In a 1940 review in the New Republic, he proclaimed that "the most impressive aspect of *The Heart is a Lonely Hunter* is the astonishing humanity that enables a white writer, for the first time in Southern fiction, to handle Negro characters with as much ease and justice as those of her own race." (Wright and Carson would later spend time together in the legendary apartment house in Brooklyn where such important artists as Leonard Bernstein, W. H. Auden, Gypsy Rose Lee, and Paul Bowles lived. Frequent visitor, writer Anais Nin, dubbed the artists haven February House because many of the tenants, like McCullers, were born in the second month of the year.)

In *Hunter*, McCullers delves deeper than the murders and riots that are the usual medium for exposing race and class injustice in literature to plumb the internal landscape of the human soul twisted by prejudice and intolerance. She also manages to dedicate an equal amount of attention to the lives of every inhabitant of the fictional town that she creates: black and white, male and female, young and old.

McCullers subdivided her house into apartments to defray the significant cost of her on-going medical expenses, with funding for those renovations provided by her friend Tennessee Williams. "I was always homesick for a place I had never seen, and now I have found it," McCullers wrote about Nyack. "It is here, this house, this town."

At the time of her death in 1967, McCullers's physician and close confidant, Dr. Mary Mercer, inherited the writer's home. When Dr. Mercer passed away on April 23, 2010, the home on South Broadway was bequeathed to the Carson McCullers Center for Writers and Musicians at Columbus State University, in Georgia. The center operates a museum in McCullers's childhood home in Columbus, presents educational and cultural programs, maintains an archive of materials about McCullers and her work, and offers fellowships for writers and composers.

"Carson McCullers came to Nyack in 1945 to convalesce and create. For 22 years she found a place to do both."

MOSELEY HALL
BASON '13

Yoga Reborn Here

Pierre Bernard, America's first yogi, lived on an ashram he called the Clarkstown Country Club in Nyack from 1920 until his death in 1955. The complex of buildings is now the campus of Nyack College. Equal parts Harry Houdini and Howard Hughes, Bernard achieved degrees of success as a yogi, animal trainer, baseball manager, and aviation expert. But millions knew him by his dubious tabloid title, Oom the Omnipotent.

A midwesterner with a flair for marketing and business savvy, Bernard was the nation's first spokesperson for yoga, a practice first mentioned in the Hindu Vedas written 3,500 years ago. As his teaching captured the imagination of enlightened European and American elites, he became a victim of his own success. The newspapers of the Hearst organization, fueling a xenophobic reaction to a wave of immigration, led a campaign to destroy Bernard's reputation.

"Pierre Bernard, America's first yogi, lived on an ashram he called the Clarkstown Country Club in Nyack from 1920 until his death in 1955."

Despite a sensationalized trial that reeked of prosecutorial misconduct and well-funded private investigations and smear campaigns, Bernard never relented. He continued to promote and teach a regimen of physical and mental conditioning that consisted of a set of specific postures, deep breathing techniques and meditation. Over time, his position prevailed. Hearst headlines went from describing his practice of yoga as an attempt to seduce "Young Girls with Hypnotic Powers" in 1910 to "Helpful to Mental, Physical Powers" in 1935.

The man the nation came to know as Oom was born Perry Arnold Baker in 1876 in Leon, Iowa. In 1889, Baker moved to Lincoln, Nebraska, next door to a Syrian Indian named Sylvais Hamati who taught Baker the physical and spiritual practice of yoga. And it was said the student kept a picture of his teacher near him for the rest of his life.

Bernard parlayed the teachings of his guru into an empire of schools, clubs, and publications that would make him millions of dollars and introduce America to yoga. But controversy accompanied each step of his steep ascent. He was literally driven from San Francisco, Seattle, and New York City by overzealous moralists using the media and public prosecutors' offices to protect conservative western values from the threat of the popular alternative teaching.

With two streams of attention converging around Bernard, muckraking journalists and affluent truth seekers, Oom the Omnipotent arrived in Nyack and spent several decades establishing his Clarkstown Country Club.

Pierre Bernard left a substantial estate to his wife and business partner Blanche De Vries. When he died in 1955, De Vries, who taught with her husband for decades, left Nyack to open a successful yoga studio in New York City. She taught into her 90s and is considered by some the First Lady of American Yoga. In 1956, De Vries sold 19 acres to what was then known as the Missionary Training Institute, now Nyack College.

One of De Vries's students, Paula Heitzner, owns and teaches at the longest running yoga studio in Nyack, the Nyack Yoga Center, founded in 1974. Her success would have pleased De Vries and Bernard. According to their biographer Robert Love, author of *The Great Oom*, "the real business was training the next generation of teachers."

In a final gesture that united his belief in physical fitness and his fondness for his home of 27 years, Bernard bequeathed the lights that illuminated the night games at his Clarkstown Country Club to the old Nyack High School sports field.

BA SON
1.24.12

MARCH 26, 2013

Couch Court

This distinctive towered structure on the corner of South Broadway and Depew was the home of the first woman to vote and practice law in Rockland County. A marker erected by the Historical Society of Rockland County records the achievements of one past inhabitant Natalie Couch, the first woman to vote in this county.

The edifice that would one day house the Couch family was built in 1854 for A. J. Storms of the Storm's Tub and Pail Factory. Mr. Storms had his house built at this location so that he could keep a watchful eye over his factory that stood on the ground that is today Memorial Park.

In the mid-19th century South Broadway was a mixed-use neighborhood, where manufacturing and agricultural properties stood side-by-side with houses. As property values rose, factories moved further inland to make room for residential development.

From 1875 until 1882 this building was the home of Edwin Stillwell, Captain of the Nyack-Tarrytown Ferry. The views from the third story must have provided a panoramic vista of the Hudson, well suited for a ship captain's residence.

The building was purchased in 1885 by the Couch Family. Dr. Louis Couch used the tower for his homeopathic practice. I thought that homeopathic remedies were a "new age" innovation of the 1960s. Apparently, homeopathy, which is a form of alternative medicine that treats patients with highly diluted preparations, found its greatest popular acceptance in the 19th century.

As fascinating as the image of men and women in period dress in a homeopath's waiting room under a pyramid-shaped roof may be, the medical practice is not the Couch family's greatest legacy.

That distinction goes to the doctor's daughter, Natalie. Natalie Couch graduated from Wellesley College in 1907 and was first in her class at Fordham Law School. In 1915, when the issue of extending the right to vote to women first appeared on the ballot in Rockland County, the measure lost by 400 votes. The initiative passed two years later and in 1918 Miss Natalie Couch became the first woman to cast a legal vote in our county. Other impressive achievements include being the first woman to:

- Practice law in Rockland County
- Serve as Journal Clerk to the New York State Assembly
- Win election as President of the Rockland County Bar Association
- Stand for election in a contest between two women (a national first)
- From 1942 to 1951, her law offices became the temporary meeting place for the New York State Supreme Court and Orangetown Town Hall, which is why this building is known by many as Couch Court.

Natalie Couch came into a world where she was legally precluded from participating in government and departed life with an obituary in the *New York Times* in 1956 that described her as New York State's Republican leader.

When you are confronted with a full accounting of Natalie Couch's life story, some legitimate questions come to mind: where is her statue, the street named in her honor, or the annual event in her name that would inspire young women to study law and enter public life? Shouldn't every young girl who walks past this building be given the boost in confidence that the telling of Natalie Couch's story would instill?

"Natalie Couch came into a world where she was legally precluded from participating in government and departed life with an obituary in the New York Times in 1956 that described her as New York State's Republican leader."

Couch Court is located at the corner of Depew Avenue and South Broadway in Nyack.

BATSON 2-2-13

FEBRUARY 5, 2013

Odd Fellows

Every time I passed this sign, I struggled to decipher the mysterious acronym. Not knowing the meaning of the hieroglyphic written in glass neon tubing gnawed at me. And when I finally obtained the answer, I was launched on another voyage of discovery. What on earth was the Independent Order of Odd Fellows and what did they do inside this building at the corner of Main and Franklin Streets? This three-story brick structure was erected in 1895 as the local lodge for the international fraternal organization. The etymology of the name is more mundane than the evocative word "odd" promises. Fraternal orders were originally organized around a particular trade, like the Freemasons, who were drawn from masons. Odd Fellows drew their members from various or "odd" trades.

The first Odd Fellows lodge was established in England in the 17th century. The group's American presence was established in Baltimore in 1819 as an altruistic social organization. When the Nyack lodge was dedicated, the Odd Fellows claimed to be the largest international fraternal organization in the world.

Support for the veracity of the boast comes from Kjeld Tideman, a painter who had a studio in the building in the 1980s and 90s. Kjeld (pronounced Shell) had a childhood memory of seeing an I.O.O.F sign in Oslo, the capital city of his native Norway. When he was setting up his painting studio, he found daguerreotypes among artifacts left behind by the group that gave the appearance that the entire white male population of Nyack belonged to the Odd Fellows.

Several facts about the Odd Fellows distinguish the group from other fraternal organizations. They were the first to accept both men and women in their ranks, and they were the first to build homes for orphans and the elderly. Illustrious past members include Ulysses S. Grant, Wyatt Earp, and Charlie Chaplin, an assortment of fellows that some might find odd.

There are still Odd Fellows organizations operating in 29 countries, but Nyack's lodge closed decades ago.

With theatrical garments, resplendent with elaborately monographed cloaks, upside- down-ice-bucket-shaped-hats, and matching collars and cuffs, the Odd Fellows are very similar to their sibling service clubs. However, they had nothing to compete with the off-beat practice of the Shriners, who appeared at public events in miniature cars. I guess if you fund children's hospitals, you amass the social equity to parade around in whatever strikes your fancy.

The man who solved the riddle of the defunct neon Odd Fellow's sign for me was Philip Biagioli. A transplant to Nyack from the Bronx, he used to pass a similar display near the Whitestone Bridge. Biagioli, who works as coordinator of media services for Rockland Community College, has his eyes on other ancient advertisements.

Biagioli would like to see the power restored to the Odd Fellows sign. The tubes that once carried illuminated neon gas in the service of spreading the Odd Fellow message have survived intact. This restoration project should not offend the purists: It doesn't need new paint, just a visit by an electrician, the flick of a switch and, voila, the gateway to our downtown business district would have a distinctive historically significant beacon. And as a landmark, Nyack can be proud of the sentiment behind the motto emblazoned on the Odd Fellow's antique electric billboard, represented by the letters F. L.T: Friendship, Love, and Truth.

"Illustrious past members include Ulysses S. Grant, Wyatt Earp and Charlie Chaplin, an assortment of fellows that some might find odd."

The IOOF building is located at the corner of Franklin Street and Main Street in Nyack.

THE OFFICE RESTAURANT
JAZZ
BATSON 6.1.12

The Office

For a brief moment in time, one of the hottest spots in the jazz universe was a nightclub in Nyack. The Office was located in the storefront that is now home to the Olde Village Inne. For five years, from 1975 until 1980 some of greatest artists of the genre, like Jaco Pastorius, Bill Evans, and many others would come to Nyack to gig at The Office. What happened at the height of the club's artistic incandescence that caused the venue to disappear from the jazz scene?

"For a brief moment in time, one of the hottest spots in the jazz universe was a nightclub in Nyack."

Michael Houghton authored a pamphlet about The Office. Houghton reported that the bar that became a Mecca for jazz musicians was only the 100th post-prohibition liquor license to be granted in New York State when it opened in 1933. He also learned that employees at the neighboring telephone company would claim that they were working late at "the office," when they were really drinking at the bar. Eventually the euphemism became the name.

In 1965, The Office was purchased by Rocco De Pietro. His son, Jack, was attending Berklee College of Music in Boston in 1975 when his father had a heart attack and considered selling the bar. But a $10,000 loan from a "regular" allowed Jack to buy a Yamaha piano and a sound system, prerequisites for a respectable jazz club, and take the helm.

According to Richard Sussman, a celebrated jazz musician and composer, The Office became a farm team for the big league jazz clubs. He described De Pietro, who was an accomplished drummer, as someone willing "to take a chance on younger, unknown players." Sussman credits The Office with giving him the opportunity to create his first quintet.

The bar was small and the stage was even smaller. The five members of Sussman's quintet would be huddled in the front of the bar with their backs to the front window. The brass section of bigger bands would be seated with the audience.

Houghton believes that The Office deserves a special place in jazz history for its interesting connection to Jaco Pastorius who revolutionized the electric bass guitar, musically and physically. By removing the frets from his electric bass he could deliver blistering streams of aggressive syncopated riffs and heart-stopping harmonics that helped transform the bass from a rhythm section to a lead instrument.

One of the instruments of the venue's meteoric rise also led to the bar's collapse. In the late 1970s, De Pietro ran regular ads on New York City jazz station WRVR that resulted in long lines of eager fans outside the club. All that changed at 10:15am on September 8, 1980, when WRVR ended its jazz era playing Charles Mingus's *Goodbye Pork Pie Hat*. The next song, Waylon Jennings's *Are You Ready for The Country*, ushered in a new country format.

Later that same week, jazz great and De Pietro family friend, Bill Evans, died days after performing at The Office. The loss of a dear friend and WRVR in the same week devastated De Pietro. Soon The Office made its own format change from jazz to blues and rock. De Pietro sold the club in 1986.

When he's returning from a late night gig in New York City, Sussman likes to drop by the Olde Village Inne, captured by the gravity of nostalgia. Or maybe there is still an invisible energy that keeps jazz music and musicians orbiting around the village where a club called The Office, like a dying star, went supernova and then silent over 30 years ago.

DA SON
2·10·13

Sam Waymon Lived Here

What do Muhammad Ali, Helen Hayes, and James Baldwin have in common? They were all guests when Sam Waymon and his creative partner, Bill Gunn, lived in this house in Nyack in the 1970s.

"What do Muhammad Ali, Helen Hayes and James Baldwin have in common? They were all guests when Sam Waymon and his creative partner, Bill Gunn lived in this house in Nyack in the 1970s."

Daniel Perry built the home in the 1830s that would eventually shelter Waymon and Gunn. Perry operated a boat building business from the property. Perry's descendants sold the property to screenwriting legend, Ben Hecht in 1929. Hecht came to Nyack to be close to his writing partner, Charles MacArthur. In a confluence that foreshadowed the activities of Waymon and Gunn, Hecht divided his time between cultural and political activities. Hecht was a major supporter of the Zionist cause and used the home for fundraising events and strategy meetings.

When Waymon and Gunn arrived in 1969, one of their first visitors was Charles MacArthur's wife, Helen Hayes, who regaled the newcomers with stories of pool parties held by the former occupants. Hayes's welcoming gesture is remembered fondly by Waymon as one of the most meaningful days at the residence, on a par with their audience with the President of Nigeria and literary gatherings that included Toni Morrison, Amiri Baraka, and Gunn's closest friend, James Baldwin.

But the most memorable and certainly most choreographed visit was from the heavyweight champion of the world. In 1975, Minister Elijah Muhammad, the founder of the Nation of Islam, learned that Gunn was being considered to write the script for an autobiographical film of the life of his disciple, Muhammad Ali. Before a deal could be struck, Gunn and Waymon were flown out to Chicago to meet with Minister Muhammad. Upon their return, they got a call from the boxer. Even though the spiritual leader had given his blessing, Ali would not agree until he met Gunn at his home. The visit was a success and work on the project proceeded.

During this period, Gunn wrote and directed *Ganja and Hess,* a film that was honored at the Cannes Film Festival in 1973 as one of the best American films of the decade. Waymon's multidisciplinary talents are on display in the film in which he performed and composed the score. As a low budget effort, many of the props and furnishings, including the Rolls Royce and the Jaguar, belonged to Waymon, and scenes were shot in and around Nyack. Gunn's prolific career as a playwright, novelist, actor, and film director ended in 1989 when he passed away at Nyack Hospital.

Waymon developed as an artist alongside his sister, celebrated songstress Nina Simone. Sam and Nina (Born Eunice Kathleen Waymon) were raised in Tyron, North Carolina, with six other brothers and sisters. Their parents, Mary Kate and John Divine, were both ministers of the gospel. Both Sam and Nina started piano lessons at the age of three. Simone recorded 40 albums and has influenced artists as diverse as Cat Stevens and Alicia Keys. During their partnership, Waymon was her manager and organist. They traveled the world performing, but they also found time to lend their talents and efforts to the civil rights movement.

In 2003, Nina Simone died in France. As a surviving sibling, Sam has been an outspoken critic of a recent Hollywood production based on his sister's life. He has been particularly critical of the casting of Zoe Saldana as Simone. Over 10,000 people signed an online petition that echo his objections. For Waymon and others, Simone's dark skin and African features defined and circumscribed her life. They are incredulous that facial prosthetics and skin paint will be employed to portray the singer.

ROCKLAND
BRINK'S
ROBBERY
BROWN
O'GRADY
PAIGE
OCTOBER 20, 1981
SOUTH
EAST
TOLL
87
287
THRUWAY
30

OCTOBER 18, 2011

The Brink's Robbery

Shared events define a community. The event has to be so overwhelming in its substance and scope that it becomes a link between strangers. In the years following a shared event, like an assassination, everyone remembers where they were when it happened. For the Rockland County community, the Brink's Robbery rises to that historic standard. On October 20, 1981, members of the Black Liberation Army robbed a Brink's truck at the Nanuet Mall. After shooting two guards, one fatally, the robbers ambushed and killed two Nyack police officers while attempting to escape over the Tappan Zee Bridge. Officers Waverly Brown and Edward O'Grady and Brink's guard, Peter Paige, lost their lives that day.

When a shared event impacts a large community like a nation, the figures involved are distant, they become blurry caricatures. Americans knew John F. Kennedy as the president with movie star good looks and Lee Harvey Oswald as the villain straight from central casting. Unlike a televised drama that you can turn off, the residents of Nyack had a front row seat to the Brink's tragedy.

As a member of a black family that has roots in Nyack going back to the 19th century, I can say the loss of Waverly Brown was very hard on us. Brown became one of the first African Americans on the Nyack Police force in 1966. He was a symbol of equality for his contemporaries and a role model for their children. That a group that purported to be fighting on behalf of African Americans caused his death is the kind of circumstance that the word ironic is inadequate to describe.

My aunt was the Deputy Village Clerk at the time of the robbery. Kathy Boudin, who was later convicted of felony murder, was handcuffed to the bench in the hallway outside her office. My aunt was anxious about going to work at the Nyack Village Hall the day after Boudin's arrest because she feared further violence. Her concerns were justified. Cognizant of the fact that the Black Liberation Army had attempted jail breaks in the past, snipers stood as sentinels on roofs of buildings along Broadway and Main Street. In October 1981, Nyack had all the hallmarks of a community under siege.

Several years after the Brink's Robbery, I became close with a childhood friend of Boudin. They had both been very active politically in the 60s before taking divergent paths. My friend became an advocate and organizer and Boudin went underground. In 1968, many activists believed that the U.S. government would eventually collapse from the mass demonstrations and riots that were sweeping the country. My friend actually bet her mother that there wouldn't be federal elections after 1968. Her mother collected on that $100 bet.

Boudin, being alienated from reality by years of living in hiding, could not accept that the government had prevailed in the counter-culture wars. Like the Japanese soldiers marooned on Pacific islands for decades after World War II, Boudin and her fellow revolutionaries did not know their movement had lost or that they were fighting for no one but themselves.

The mood of discontent and tumult that hovered over our nation during the 1960s had drained away by the afternoon of October 20, 1981. The Vietnam War was over, a stubborn truce had held between racial antagonists and an era of upheaval gave way to a period of relative calm. The storm of violence on that day fell with no warning from a clear blue sky. But instead of a whole nation being deluged, the full downpour of despair fell only on the Village of Nyack.

"The storm of violence on that day fell with no warning from a clear blue sky. But instead of a whole nation being deluged, the full downpour of despair fell only on the Village of Nyack."

A memorial is located at the corner of Route 59 and Mountainview Avenue in Central Nyack at the site of the shooting.

O'Donoghue's
O'Donoghue's
ZEPPA 2
TAVERN
Lite
Kitchen
Open
2-10pm

JUNE 24, 2014

O'Donoghue's Tavern

For 62 of the last 64 years, the pub near the corner of Main Street and Broadway in Nyack has been owned by an O'Donoghue. There has been an O'Donoghue behind the bar since 1949, when Paul O'Donoghue Sr. started working as a night barman for what was then called Charlie's Bar & Grill. After Charlie Lindell's death in 1960, his wife, Hilda, sold the bar to Paul. This May, Paul O'Donoghue's son, Kevin, returned to the helm of the bar after a two year hiatus.

O'Donoghue's Tavern is where many had their first drink or first date. For generations, 66 Main Street has been the venue for formal and informal bachelor and bachelorette parties, high school reunions and anniversaries. For over a century there has been an adult community center on this site serving liquid recreation and comfort food. If you wanted to go where everybody knew your name in Nyack, you went to O'D's.

"I've been going to O'D's since I was in high school," Pickwick Book Shop owner Jack Dunnigan reminisced. He is well acquainted with the tavern business; his family operated the beloved Dunnigan's Bar and Grill in West Haverstraw for decades. "I wanted to branch out from Haverstraw, so I came to Nyack," said Dunnigan. "Mr. and Mrs. O'Donoghue would treat you like family. There was a certain degree of decorum that was expected and if you went beyond that point, they would let you know. They never had to remind me, of course. And when you left, Paul Sr. would always say "g'night, g'night" or "next time bring money," Dunnigan fondly recalled.

Upon hearing Jack's recollection, Kevin O'Donoghue said, "He's lying," as he lifted the corner of his mouth to form a playful smile. "Jack started coming here in grade school."

A more solemn example of the family feeling that many associate with O'Donoghue's is from the aftermath of the Brink's robbery in 1980, when Nyack police officers Edward O'Grady and Waverly "Chip" Brown were shot down.

"Everything was closed in town the day after the shooting, but there were hundreds of firefighters and cops who came to Nyack and had nowhere to go, so my father opened the bar. He served them, but he wouldn't take any money. When they left that first night, the bar was covered in cash, so he gathered it up, and brought it to the police station and told them to give it to the widows and orphans fund," said O'Donoghue.

"A few weeks later, the Emerald Society Marching Band walked through our doors circling around my mother and father as they sat in the back. I remember my mother crying," O'Donoghue continued. "Phil Caruso, the Police Benevolent Association President, gave my father an honorary shield."

Kevin's plans for the future are expressed in simple terms, "I am very happy to be back with all my friends. My plan is to enjoy life."

With the brevity that is the soul of wit, a sign on the door says it all: "O'D's is under 'new' old management."

"For 62 of the last 64 years, the pub near the corner of Main Street and Broadway in Nyack has been owned by an O'Donoghue."

O'Donoghue's is located at 66 Main Street, Nyack.

BATSON 12-15-11
PICKWICK
BOOK
SHOP
EUROPEAN CH

Pickwick Book Shop

San Francisco has City Lights, New York City has The Strand, and Nyack has the Pickwick Book Shop. The experience of shopping at Pickwick has changed little since it first opened in 1945. A seemingly infinite number of titles are crammed into a dense thicket of shelves. Books cover the floor and walls, arching as they approach the ceiling in ponderously tall stacks, in the way that trees canopy in a rain forest. At the center of this untamed landscape of literature is Pickwick's owner, Jack Dunnigan.

Jack wears thick round glasses and sports a bushy white mustache. He has the air of a rumpled history teacher. He hovers above his inventory on a slightly elevated rostrum-like platform. Behind him are hundreds of books bound with rubber bands that contain the names of certain customers. When you express an interest in a book not on the shelf, Jack makes a note and the next time you arrive you are handed the sought after volume.

Anyone who has been to Pickwick leaves with more than just a book. My drawing is a homage to the distinctive black-and-white bookmark created by John Richards that accompanies every sale. Richards created similar iconic logos for Christopher's and the Hudson House of Nyack. Jack estimates that he has distributed over 250,000 bookmarks since the first printing in the late 80s.

Despite the proximity of bookstore chains at the Nanuet and Palisades Center Malls, Pickwick endures. I have been shopping at Pickwick since the early 70s when I bought my first book with my own money: an illustrated version of Bram Stoker's *Dracula*.

Pickwick is not just a local headquarters for bibliophiles. Jack divides his time between managing his shop and organizing the Art, Craft, and Antique Dealers of Nyack (ACADA). First organized in 1971, ACADA sponsors three of the five street fairs that Nyack hosts annually. The events are so popular that they quadruple the population of the village for the day, bringing in revenue and establishing Nyack as a regional destination. The longevity of Pickwick would be sufficiently satisfying to most, but Jack has a restless interest in improving the fortunes of his fellow merchants.

Jack is driven by an appreciation for local history that is anchored in the bedrock of our community, literally. Jack's family ran a brickworks in northern Rockland County. His family converted the brickyard's watering hole into the beloved Dunnigan's Bar & Grill in West Haverstraw.

Wanting to expand Jack's intellectual horizons, Frank Dunnigan would bring Jack and his brothers to visit Pickwick at its original location on Main Street. Jack remembers the thrill he felt visiting the county's only bookstore, named after the first novel by Charles Dickens. In 1975, Jack acquired the shop from Herbert Sperkkber. At the time, Suffern and Piermont had bookstores. Only Nyack has kept the doors of a local bookstore open.

City Lights won landmark status this May. We should move to landmark the spot where Helen Hayes signed books one Mother's Day, where Frank McCourt attracted a mob on a cold Friday night, and where Carson McCullers was spotted hunting alone for reading material. The commercial viability of Pickwick is more than just a matter of picking sides between national vs. local bookstores, or cyber vs. brick and mortar book shopping. If we fail to support one of Nyack's most distinguished businesses, we risk becoming indistinguishable from other communities ourselves.

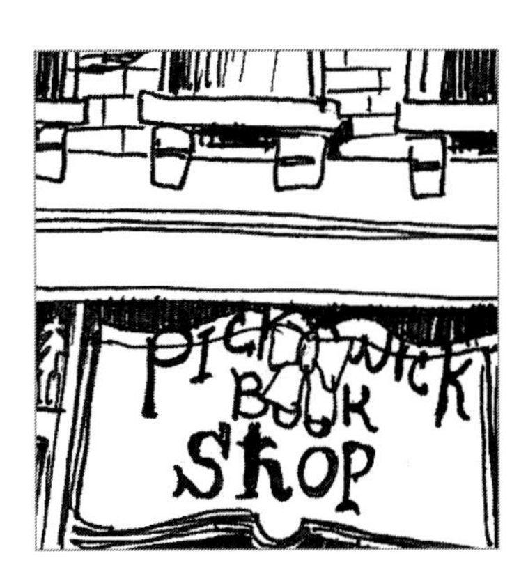

"San Francisco has City Lights, New York City has the Strand and Nyack has the Pickwick Book Shop."

Pickwick is located at 8 South Broadway, Nyack.

KOBLIN'S PHARMACY
Back To School Center
HELP WANTED
INQUIRE WITHIN
THEATRE
BALSON 9.9.12

SEPTEMBER 11, 2012

Koblin's Pharmacy

Jerry Koblin works his age. The owner of Koblin's Pharmacy turned 75 last month, and he works that number of hours every week. Since he took over the family business from his father in the late 1960s, Jerry has been a driving force in the civic and commercial life of Nyack. And with the recent arrival of the national pharmacy chain Walgreens, Jerry has no plans to close shop or cut back on his hours.

Koblin's is not the first pharmacy to dispense medicine and merchandise from this address on Main Street. In 1890, John D. Blauvelt relocated his Spring Valley apothecary to Nyack in an effort to create the most exclusive drug store in Rockland County. The interior looked more like a soda shop than a pharmacy and the staff more like waiters than health care workers.

In 1934, Jerry's father bought the business from the Blauvelts and continued filling the community's prescriptions. Jerry's first position in his father's store was as a stock runner, resupplying the shelves from the cavernous storage space in the basement as products were sold. After his graduation from the University of Connecticut and six years in the Air National Guard, which included a year and a half at Andrews Air Force base, he brought his pharmacist's license back to Nyack.

Jerry's father was ambivalent about passing on the torch to his son. "He pleaded with me not to do this" Jerry told me. His father warned him that the obligation was seven days a week and 365 days a year. But Jerry looked at his father and saw a man that everybody liked and respected. "I never thought about doing anything else." But he also acknowledges that his old man was right about the nature of the commitment.

The health care system that prompted Jerry's father's admonition was profoundly less complex and litigious than his son has experienced since he took over. In 1970, people paid for their medicine out of pocket. There were no health insurance companies and no computerized records. Most prescriptions cost between $4 and $6 to fill. Jerry vividly remembers the first time a third party paid the cost of someone's medication.

In the last nine years, Jerry has seen the cost of prescription medication skyrocket. He feels the impact of this escalation as a retailer, as well as an employer who provides health insurance for his nine full-time employees. "We have one product that used to cost $6 a tube that now costs $100."

In March of 2014, Jerry sold the pharmacy to Jeffrey Rucker, who has continued to provide employment to the staff that loyally served alongside Jerry Koblin for decades. For the last 80 years, a pharmacy called Koblin's has filled prescriptions on Main Street and, under Rucker's leadership, it will continue.

"For the last 80 years, a pharmacy called Koblin's filled prescriptions on Main Street."

Koblin's is located at 96 Main Street, Nyack.

Maria Luisa
BATSON 2014

AUGUST 5, 2014

Maria Luisa

Maria Luisa Whittingham is a civic seamstress. She weaves business, social responsibility, and family into a garment of retail longevity. From the durable and colorful threads of a matriarchal tradition and her own raw talent, she has created a popular business and brand: *Maria Luisa.*

"Maria Luisa Whittingham is a civic seamstress, weaving business, social responsibility and family into a garment of retail longevity."

Where did you learn the merchant tradition?

My first experience with the merchant tradition was very early on in my life. My mother, Carmen Mercedes Colon de Perez, had a bazaar in Cayey, Puerto Rico. I grew up exploring the back rooms and looking under the cases of her general store.

She started the store when she was in her 20s. She had an eighth-grade education. When her mother died, she had to go to work and help the family as the eldest. She worked for a department store as their bookkeeper and manager. When she opened her own store, she carried everything from soap to thread to handbags to dresses.

So your mother was your mentor?

She was my hugest supporter. She was definitely my mentor. For someone with little opportunity, she really maximized what she had. Later in her life, as a stay-at-home mother, she sewed. She was also a great seamstress. I would sit under her sewing machine and take her scraps and sew. No lessons. I would just get a needle and thread and sew clothes right onto my dolls.

When we moved to the States in 1967, I was in fifth grade. I started sewing my clothes and by middle school, classmates were paying me $15 to embellish their jeans.

What was your first job in fashion?

The first job I had was with London Fog. I was doing rain coats. One of my professors, Mary Ann Ferro, worked there and recommended me. I went to work at 512 Seventh Avenue, the coat building.

Where was your first store?

I started downstairs in the mall next to the YMCA in 1987. I started with $2,000. I was 30 years old. Everything I sold, I made. I fashioned ribbons into belts, I made silk blouses, lace lingerie. It was half the size of my current back room. After two moves inside of the mall at 37 South Broadway, I took the leap and opened on the corner of Burd Street and South Broadway where I stayed for 21 years, until I moved to my current locations at 77 and 75 South Broadway.

Tell me about Maria Luisa Global/Local.

ML G/L provides merchandise that empowers globally and locally. I purchase items that empower women in a village in Africa, or Latin America, or Asia, or a community here in the United States. Some of my vendors are not-for-profit companies, like Malia Designs, that use the profits from their sales to reduce human trafficking around the world. The products that they make use already existing materials that are made by communities that are getting empowered also by crafting the product. One example is a bag made from recycled cement bags made in Cambodia.

Eventually, when you purchase a product from ML G/L on our website, you will be able to direct a portion of the proceeds to a local non-profit, like the Nyack Center. ML G/L is a way to give back locally, while supporting communities globally.

Maria Luisa is located at 75 & 77 S. Broadway, Nyack.

VILLAGE HALL
NYACK-ON-HUDSON
FIRE
FIRE
Nyack

MARCH 19, 2013

Mayor Jen Laird-White

In recognition of Women's History Month, *Nyack Sketch Log* talks with Village of Nyack Mayor, Jen Laird-White about the state of the village and the high and low points of her first term and her future plans.

Are there any particular blessings or burdens for women in public office?
Holding public office is no different for men or women today. It's equally tough for everyone because there has been such a breach in the public trust. This is, however, an exciting moment to be in public life because everywhere you look women are taking on leadership roles in business and government.

"This is, however, an exciting moment to be in public life because everywhere you look women are taking on leadership roles in business and government."

Are there any women in politics that inspire you?
Recently, I have had a chance to work closely with our member of Congress, Nita Lowey. I am amazed by her work ethic, passion, and fearlessness. She is a total inspiration and we are lucky to have her representing us in Congress.

What has been the low point of your term?
The low point was Hurricane Sandy. The devastation was stunning. In the immediate aftermath, relief was not easy or forthcoming. During the storm and in the horrible days right after, we lost power, we sustained substantial damage as a community, and we lost a life. It was a terrifically difficult time. But our community spirit and resolve was kept afloat by our first responders who tirelessly and without complaint went about saving lives and working to maintain order and restore services.

The high point?
There were actually some high points during those bleak days. The Village Hall steps provided a gathering spot. One neighbor was more generous than the next. There were guys from Georgia who left their homes and families to patrol our streets to restore power. Even as people suffered their own loss and anxiety, they reached out to others during those meetings. The selflessness was incredible.

What is the state of the village?
I am proud to say that the state of Nyack is very strong, despite the continued struggles of small towns across the nation. The village finances are in the best shape they have been in for decades. The taxpayers actually have a substantial savings account. It's a reserve for the unexpected.

Our waterfront and, in particular, our marina were devastated by Hurricane Sandy. That said, we have hired an amazing new recreation director, Melody Partrick, who is working on programming our park so that our residents have recreation activities here in their own backyard. There is an incredible and active group of parents who are raising money through the Nyack Park Conservancy for an impressive new playground, and the Park Commission is working on plans for a new garden near the playground.

Any Tappan Zee Bridge updates?
As a member of the Governor's Transit Task Force, I am committed to finding viable transit options for Rockland. I think we need to work closely with South Nyack and Grandview, the two communities who will struggle most during the construction phase, to determine what they need for construction survival and what all of our needs are for transit in the future.

How is your family surviving your public responsibilities?
Patiently. My rather quiet husband, Richard, has had to learn to gab a bit more and my boys, Jack and Luke, can't really get in trouble because everyone knows their mother.

Nyack Village Hall is located at 9 North Broadway, Nyack.

NAACP's Frances Pratt

Elegant hats have become the symbol of local civil rights icon, Frances Pratt. But when she arrived at the Port Authority Bus Terminal in New York City 60 years ago, she wore a borrowed dress and shoes too tight for walking.

Pratt grew up with her mother, four sisters, and two brothers in rural South Carolina. An incident from her early childhood shaped her future activism. "I walked into an ice-cream parlor with my mother and the clerk said, 'You can buy the ice cream, but you have to eat outside.' I had never seen my mother demeaned in that way. If she had spoken up, the clerk would have called the police."

"Elegant hats have become the symbol of local civil rights icon Frances Pratt."

In May 1955, Frances, who was attending Friendship College in Rock Hill, South Carolina, learned that she would not be returning to school. "My mother sat me down and said 'you are going to have to go to work for a while,'" Pratt recalled. "My brother, Billy Powell, and my mother were not well." With the support of a teacher, Pratt found a potential employer in New York who would pay her $40 per month that she could send home to support the family. She first had to travel to Clover, South Carolina, to pick peaches to raise the $17.50 for her bus fare.

Two years after arriving in New York City, Frances moved to South Nyack into the home of new husband Marshall Pratt. "I met Marshall in Mount Morris Park in Harlem while I was on a field trip with a group of children," said Pratt. "I was working for a nursery school founded by Dr. Thelma Adair, the first woman to serve as an elected Moderator for the Presbyterian Church. Marshall declared that he wore out four tires circling the park trying to see me again. When he found me, we made a date."

When Pratt came to Nyack, she dreamed of attending the missionary program at Nyack College. "I wanted to go to Addis Ababa in Africa." But responsibilities to family required that she find a way to serve the world closer to home, so she enrolled in Rockland Community College where she obtained her degree in nursing. Pratt went on to work at Nyack Hospital for 53 years, holding titles including Head Nurse of the Emergency Room and the Office of Employee Health.

This week's sketch is based on a photo that currently hangs in the emergency room lobby of Nyack Hospital. The lobby, as well as a scholarship and a Peace Rose Garden, were named in her honor when she retired. "What I appreciate most about this recognition is that it is not about the late Frances Ethel Powell Pratt. I can actually read the plaque and smell the roses!"

In 1981, Pratt was elected President of the local branch of the NAACP. On Thursday night, April 25, Pratt will host the organization's annual fundraising gala at the Pearl River Hilton. While all eyes will be focused on this year's keynote speaker, New York State NAACP President, Hazel Dukes, people will find it difficult to turn away from Pratt, who always appears in a hat more spectacular than the previous year.

Pratt credits her husband, Marshall, who passed away in 2002, for her memorable hats. "My husband designed all my hats. He was a talented artist and would always design my hats and coordinate my outfits." In 2005, Pratt's collection of 250 *chapeaux* were on display at Rockland Community College for a fundraising event for the NAACP.

5
HOSE
1910
85
BATSON 6·30·12

Nyack Fire Department

For as long as I can remember, each time the fire whistle sounded, someone in our household would grab the dog-eared laminated chart held to the refrigerator by a magnet. The chart had the key to decode the location of each Fire Department call. Every household in the village receives a calendar from the Fire Department during the second week of October each year, a tradition that goes back to 1927.

Vigorous public discussion about the need for fire whistles is almost as old as the department itself. In the 19th century, alarms were raised by ringing a massive bell that once stood in front of the Mazeppa Fire House on Main Street. When the bell was finally retired to the tower of the North campus of Nyack College, a device known as the Mocking Bird took its place until steam power became obsolete. The current electronic whistle initially repeated the fire signal four times, but after opposition from neighbors adjacent to the firehouse, the number was reduced by two.

In an era of increasing reliance on wireless communication, some have predicted the demise of the fire whistle. But recent catastrophes have demonstrated that our dependence on complex electronic systems can leave us vulnerable. During blackouts, landlines, mobile phones, and Internet services are useless. In a prolonged power outage, a generator-powered air whistle may be the only reliable means of emergency communication.

Another advent of the modern era, the electronic fire alarm, is also a mixed blessing to the fire department. With increasing frequency, volunteers race to false alarms caused by faulty computerized fire safety systems. Because every alarm must be investigated, false alarms expose volunteers to danger as they needlessly rush to the scenes where there is no real emergency. False alarms also waste limited fire fighting resources.

Rockland is the last county in New York State to have a 100% volunteer fire department and Nyack's Fire Department is the oldest in the county. Most people would need to be coerced or conscripted into risking their lives or require some form of compensation to leave their jobs and their families. Not our volunteer fire fighters! Sadly, the future of the volunteer service is at risk as fewer people are stepping forward to serve.

Only two graduates in the latest class from the Rockland Country Fire Training Center will be joining the Nyack department. Starting young seems to be the secret to the longevity of a volunteer.

Nyack Joint Fire District Chairman, Keith Taylor, and Nyack Fire Department Chief, Jim Petriello, both started volunteering in their teens and have a combined 70 years of service. In a wonderful oral history, Everett "Smokey" Wanamaker describes 60 years of membership in the Empire Hook and Ladder Company in Upper Nyack that started when he was 16.

The fire whistle alerts your neighbors who volunteer that there is a fire to fight. We are fortunate to have their service and a reliable system to organize their actions on our behalf. Unlike a cell phone that can be lost, lose battery power, or be set on vibrate, the fire whistle cannot be ignored. And when it's your house that is on fire, you'll pray for and want the prompt attention of our fire-fighting cavalry.

"Rockland is the last county in New York State to have a 100% volunteer fire department and Nyack's Fire Department is the oldest in the county."

If you want to become a volunteer or make a contribution to the Nyack Fire Department visit nyackfire.org.

THE HUDSON HOUSE OF NYACK

AUGUST 28, 2012

Hudson House

May 2012 was a big month at the Hudson House, one of Nyack's premier restaurants. *The New York Times* praised new chef, Jeffrey Kaufman, for his "dazzling dishes." And owners Matt Hudson and Amy Lehman received an award for Historic Preservation from Rockland County Executive Scott Vanderhoef. In both culinary standards and civic responsibility, the Hudson House is getting high marks, which is fitting when you are serving the public from a building that was once the Village Hall.

From 1881 until 1970, Nyack's trustees and magistrates deliberated and passed judgment in the two-story brick building at 134 Main Street. Architectural elements from the original building, like stamped tin walls and ceilings, are still in pristine condition. The space where jail cells once stood to dry out winos is now used to incarcerate wine bottles.

"The space where jail cells once stood to dry out winos is now used to incarcerate wine bottles."

Nyack's government vacated the building in the 1970s. Since then, three eateries have opened shop on the spot. The Pasione twins operated a luncheonette on the first floor that lasted for several years. A Soho restaurateur purchased the building in 1981, undertook extensive renovations, and opened Raoul's Village Hall Restaurant.

That same year, Matt Hudson was tending bar in Westchester. Hudson, the eighth of ten children, followed his brother Eddie into the hospitality business. His parents moved the family to Rockland County from the Bronx in 1950, with 12 like-minded neighbors, to establish a utopian, catholic community called Marycrest in West Nyack. His mother, Dorothy, not only managed to feed her large family, but she instilled in them a love for cooking that led seven of her children to spend a major part of their careers in the food industry.

When the establishment where Matt worked began to falter, he approached his brother Eddie's boss, Serge Raoul, about a management position in his Nyack restaurant. Hudson was advised that the position required that he be available seven days a week. If he was going to work that hard, Hudson reasoned, he would rather buy the business and work for himself.

Hudson House manager, Skye O'Jea Spiegel, worked with Matt in Westchester and decided to join the couple when they opened their new restaurant. Pedro Reyes, who previously worked for Raoul, stayed on to help them launch the new venture. The team has stuck together for over two decades.

It takes a lot of creativity as well as persistence to succeed in the restaurant business. Matt is a photographer and sculptor and his business partner, Amy Lehman, is a professional dancer and choreographer. Many of Matt's black-and-white portraits of family and friends and lush landscapes of the Hudson River are on display and give the restaurant its river village ambiance.

One measure of their success is that Matt has taken out his wood chisels and started to sculpt again. He had set aside his tools for almost 30 years to focus on work. The bar of the Hudson House features three large wooden bas-reliefs of design features from the Federal building on Church Street in Manhattan. Two other pieces are recreations of NYC manhole covers, one representational, one surreal.

In a small town, a popular restaurant is like a civic center. As they approach their 23rd anniversary, the Hudson House of Nyack is more than a place to eat, it's a local institution. Because the Nyack community values historic preservation, art, fine food, and hospitality, Hudson House is right at home.

Hudson House is located at 134 Main Street, Nyack.

Maura's Kitchen
Peruvian & Latin American Home Cooking

MARCH 20, 2012

Maura's Kitchen

When she receives compliments for her cooking, Maura Azanedo has been known to say "I am not a chef, I am a cook." Home cooking, with all the feelings of fullness and satisfaction that the term conveys, is what Maura's Kitchen promises and delivers.

Maura arrived in the United States from Peru in 1970 to attend high school in Kentucky as a foreign exchange student. Job opportunities and the desire to master English brought her to New York, where she met her husband Edwin in the tight-knit Peruvian community in Washington Heights. They moved to Rockland County in 1995.

"When I was growing up, I couldn't go out much at night because dinner was important and I had to be home," says Maura's and Edwin's son, Tyrone. I imagine that it wasn't just parental admonition that kept Tyrone at the table. The food that his mother cooked for her family was so phenomenal that both father and son urged her to open a restaurant.

Maura didn't learn her cooking chops from a culinary school, which is why she insists she's more cook than chef, having learned her way around the kitchen from aunts and a grandmother in Lima, Peru. Her father, Alberto Haro, a prominent figure in the Peruvian folk music genre, *Musica Criolla,* was always on the road. It was during his extended absences that four aunts and a grandmother gave young Maura her kitchen training.

When the Azanedos opened Maura's Kitchen in March 2011, they were afraid that an over emphasis on Peruvian cuisine might turn away diners. The sign they hung expresses that ambivalence offering Peruvian "and Latin American" cooking. "We were shocked that from day one, some of the people who came into the store knew as much about Peru as we did," said Edwin. Even more startling and serendipitous was how Peruvian cuisine exploded onto the culinary scene in 2011.

Thanks to super star chef Gaston Acurio, there is a growing global obsession with Peruvian food. References to Acurio as the ambassador to Peruvian food would seem like title inflation if not for the fact that he runs 28 restaurants in 12 countries. The recently opened La Mar Cebicheria in NYC was his 29th, a launch "god-fathered" by renowned chef, Danny Meyer.

A sign outside a restaurant proclaiming "Home Cooking" can be deceptive: you may get healthy portions, but there's no guarantee that the food will approach the authenticity we expect from that proclamation. That's not the case at Maura's where the mother runs the kitchen, the father stands behind the cash register, and the son promotes the business. The cuisine that the foodie world is now embracing as a formal phenom is available right here in the village, minus the pretense, in an environment that will make you feel right at home.

Less than a year after this column was posted, Maura's husband, Edwin Azanedo, suffered a fatal heart attack while working at the restaurant. As a constant presence behind the counter, Edwin became a beloved feature of this family-run, family restaurant. His wife, Maura, and their son, Tyrone, have kept the business and continue to receive the support of their loyal customers.

When she receives compliments for her cooking, Maura Azanedo has been known to say "I am not a chef: I am a cook."

Maura's Kitchen is located at 248 Main Street, Nyack.

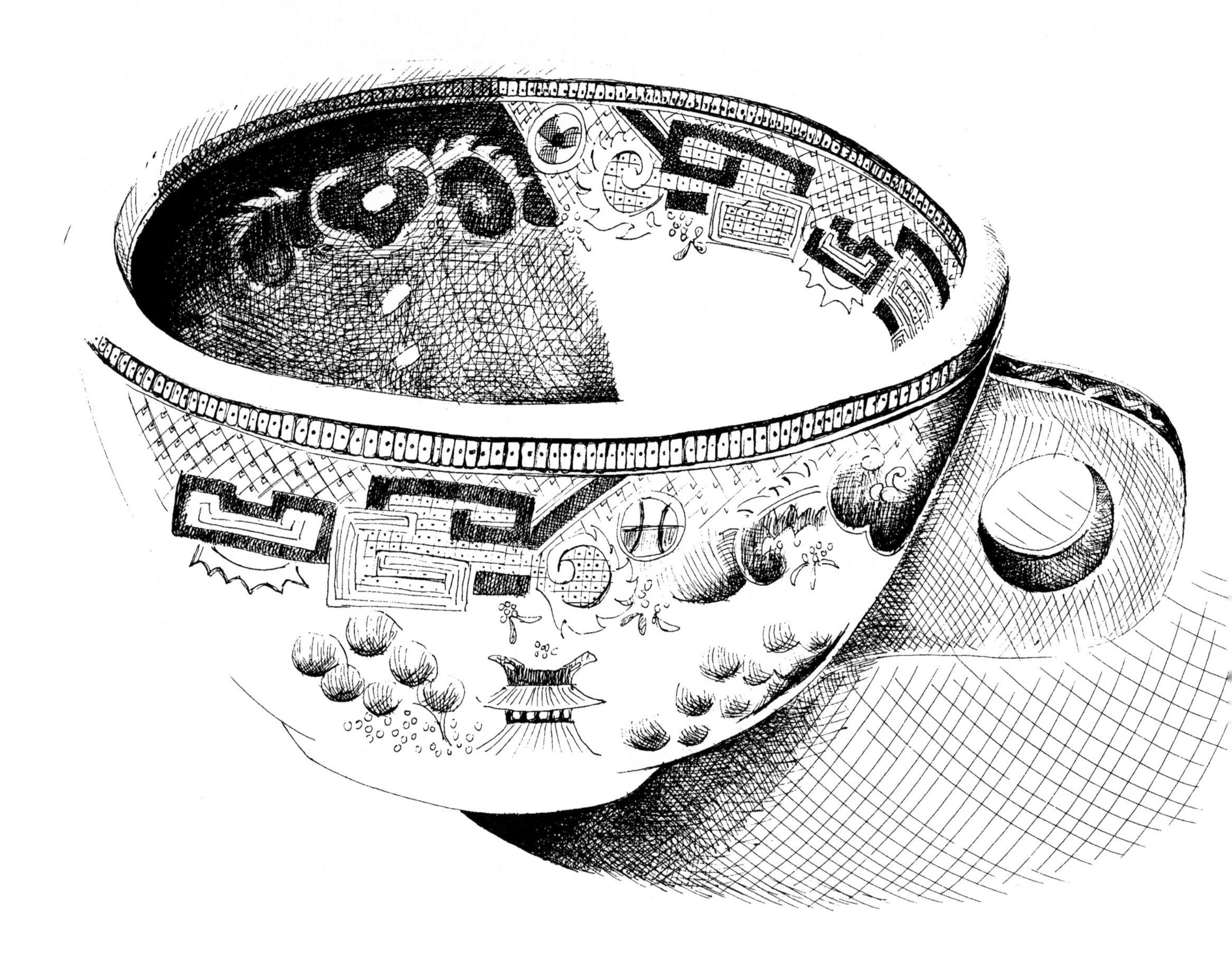

Preston Powell's Teagevity

During his journey from Harlem to Martha's Vineyard to Nyack, Preston Powell has melded a teacup, karate, and a tradition of the African American church from his childhood into his holistic and locally based business, Teagevity.

Tell me about this teacup?

When I was about 19 or 20, I walked into a martial arts dojo on Lexington Ave. in New York City and saw a man, who turned out to be the Sensei, holding a cup of tea. The way he held that teacup struck me. It reminded me of my childhood, when women would sit for tea after services at Abyssinian Baptist Church. When I started my martial arts training, everything was about holding a cup of tea—your posture, your movement, you had to defend a teacup. Eventually, I was given this teacup. For over twenty years, I have protected this cup. It has been my introduction to Asian and other tea-drinking cultures. It is a connection to the fellowship of drinking tea after church.

"Preston Powell has melded a teacup, Karate and a tradition of the African American church from his childhood into his holistic and locally based business, Teagevity."

What is your connection to Abyssinian Baptist Church?

My grandfather was Adam Clayton Powell Jr. He was pastor of Abyssinian Baptist Church in Harlem and, in 1945, he was the first African American from New York State elected to Congress. My grandmother, Isabel Washington Powell, was a dancer at the Cotton Club when she met and married Adam Clayton Powell. I am in the process of donating some items from my family to the Smithsonian Institution in Washington, D.C., for their new African American Wing. One of the exhibits is going to be about early black residents on Martha's Vineyard. My grandparents summered and owned a cottage there.

How did you come to Nyack?

As a child, I spent my summers by the water in Martha's Vineyard. I also spent a lot of time in Sag Harbor, N.Y. When I came across the Tappan Zee Bridge one day, around 1999, and I saw the Village of Nyack and the Hudson River, I instantly knew this would be a home for my family.

When did you open your dojo?

To-te Ueshiro Karate Club opened in 2006. It is organized as a club more than a business. We don't advertise, we don't have a neon sign. The focus is on training for personal growth, not for competition or trophies. In our Shorin-Ryu tradition, skills are handed down through the family. We try to prepare the father to train the daughter and the grandfather to train with the grandson. It's an activity for the whole family. Our style of karate was brought to Okinawa, Japan, by men who were taught by Shaolin monks in China. They were in Okinawa as traders and taught their trading partners martial arts to protect themselves from the mainland Japanese. My teacup came from Japan.

When did you launch Teagevity?

I was frustrated with the business of music, and I wanted to create something new and local that my family could be a part of. Tea had been on my mind. I loved the substance of it and the rituals around it. In the dojo, students would ask what to do when they didn't feel well. I had become an elder dispensing wisdom about medicinal properties of different teas and herbs. Then one day, when I was driving with my wife and saying how much I loved life, she said the word longevity, and then added the word tea. When I heard "Teagevity," that was it. I got the domain name that day. Now, a year later, I carry 54 varieties of tea.

For more information visit teagevity.com.

BATSON
5-27-12

NOVEMBER 26, 2013

The Pie Lady & Son

Deborah Tyler had 300 pie orders to fill in the Fall of 2001. The single mother of three had converted her one floor rental into a Department of Health-approved commercial kitchen. A *New York Times* review and a Good Morning America segment were bringing in business from both sides of the Hudson River. It was at the height of her notoriety that Deborah sold her equipment and moved to Cooperstown, N.Y. Here is the story of how the popularity of their pies once imperiled The Pie Lady and now propels The Pie Lady & Son.

From 1995 until 2001, if you were in the know, or you stumbled upon the hand-painted sign that said "Pie" on Piermont Avenue in Nyack and followed the arrow, you would have arrived at Tyler's back porch. If it was a busy day, she might have her youngest daughter, Carly, under her arm as she took your order. If apple pie is the closest thing we have to a national dish, serving the iconic dessert from a kitchen door is pure Americana.

When she moved to Burd Street she was on her own with three young children. Baking was a way to earn Tyler some extra money. But as soon as the sign went up on the corner of Piermont and Burd, word of mouth drove business in her direction faster than Deborah could manage. Her brother helped convert her son Wil's bedroom into an extra kitchen. Her upstairs neighbor offered additional space.

The village gave Tyler her name. She tried in vain to get people to call her business "The Pie Kitchen." But from the moment she started selling baked goods from her back porch she would be affectionately known as "The Pie Lady."

The Pie Lady would eventually become a victim of her own rapid growth. As the orders poured in, she wanted a business partner to appear, someone to handle the administration, leaving her to the baking. But a culinary comrade never emerged. The only thing that arrived was more business. By 2001, exhausted and unable to keep up with the demand, Tyler closed shop and moved to Cooperstown.

Her son, Wil, who gave up his bedroom years earlier to allow for kitchen expansion, immediately wanted his mother to reconsider. He took a job in marketing out of high school, but his heart was with the family business. Wil converted his mother's recipes from index cards to computer files and traveled to Cooperstown for baking lessons. He also convinced his sister, Briana, to obtain a certificate to bake in his apartment.

Wil and Briana's efforts were enthusiastically welcomed when baked goods labeled "Pie Lady" were spotted at the St. Ann's Holiday Bazaar in 2009. Their next step was to open a booth at the Nyack Chamber of Commerce's Farmers' Market in 2010. The siblings were making 30 pies a week and were feeling quite proud of the results. They outgrew Wil's apartment and were working out of rented kitchen space at the Fellowship of Reconciliation, when Deborah came to check on their progress. She was impressed by their zeal, but not as pleased with the product. Since that visit, Deborah has made a weekly trip back to Nyack to oversee production.

There is nothing secret about the Tyler recipe for baking or success. Community support is like yeast, the love of family is the filling, and the crust is just the right proportion of flour, water, salt, and fat. The reign of The Pie Lady is over: long live The Pie Lady & Son!

"Here is the story of how the popularity of their pies once imperiled the Pie Lady and now propels the Pie Lady & Son."

366 N. Highland Avenue
Upper Nyack

BATSON 6.7.12

Year-Round Farmers' Market

Each Thursday morning at 6:00am, over a dozen vendors arrive in the municipal parking lot in Nyack. Two hours later, a tent village has risen from the asphalt. Every week, crates of locally-grown produce and boxes of fresh baked goods are presented for sale on folding tables. Since May 10th, 2012 I have recorded this vibrant expression of the commercial life of our village as the first artist-in-residence for Nyack's Farmers' Market.

"The Nyack Farmers' Market operates from the Main Municipal parking lot from April to November, and from December through March it operates at the Nyack Center, at the corner of Depew and South Broadway."

Nyack's Farmers' Market is a project of the Nyack Chamber of Commerce. Launched in 1979 in Veteran's Park by Carol Baxter, the market has had various managers, including Lorie Reynolds and one-time Chamber Board member Art Clark. Currently, the market is supervised by Chamber Board member, Carlo Pellegrini, and managed by Pam Moskowitz.

Pellegrini estimates that up to 1,000 shoppers visit the market each Thursday. From its inception, the mission of the market has been to surpass the noble goal of providing quality goods at reasonable prices. Pellegrini sees the market as "a place where folks come to meet and greet each other and catch up on news of each others' lives and the Village."

As proud as Pellegrini is of the role that the Chamber plays in operating the market, the very spelling of the name of the market reflects the driving force behind the venture. Farmers' is purposely spelled *s'*, not *'s*, because this is truly the market of the farmers who show up every week," Pellegrini said.

In collaboration with the Nyack Center, there is now a winter market from December through March. The establishment of an indoor market was the brainchild of a farmer, Richard Concklin of The Orchards of Concklin, this market's first and longest-serving vendor.

Live musical performance distinguishes Nyack's Farmers' Market. Spring and summer afternoons have the feel of a county fair when performing artists like the Bossy Frog Band and Mario the Magician attract families to downtown Nyack for a show, a chance to mingle with friends, and an opportunity to shop.

Historically, communal markets have been a civilizing force in the evolution of human society. Every culture on every continent has developed strikingly similar forums were people who produce goods seek consumers. Whether the venue was as basic as the shade of a large tree, or a built structure with permanent stalls, these markets became the center of community life.

The marketplace has played a pivotal role in the social and financial organization of our civilization. Our economy, referred to as a market-based system, was modeled on the dynamic of individuals entering a market to compete for the best value for commodities. The word "bank" comes from the Italian word for bench, *banco*: the surface from which the practices that would become our modern banking system were pioneered in medieval markets.

Gradually, through the centuries, fixed public markets, like London's Covent Garden or the West Side Market in Cleveland, Ohio, were eventually superseded by commercial districts, shopping centers, and finally, the malls.

However, over the last 25 years, the farmers' market movement has reasserted some of the values of the ancient marketplace where people bought their food directly from the growers. This more direct exchange between consumer and producer removes the added expense and waste created by the armies of middlemen who profit from packaging, shipping, displaying, advertising, and re-selling agricultural goods.

BASON 7·14·12

The Orchards of Concklin

Since Nicholas Concklin sought to have the land that he farmed named *Pomona*, after the Roman goddess of fruitful abundance, eleven generations of Concklins have tilled the soil in Rockland County. The Orchards of Concklin is the oldest family business in New York State and the eighth oldest in the country.

Over 100 neighbors, customers, and relatives gathered on July 4th, 2012 at the Orchards of Concklin, at the intersection of Route 45 and South Mountain Road in Pomona, to celebrate their tricentennial. Linda Concklin, the farm store manager, spoke of the role that the community has played in their longevity. "We are still here because of all of you," was her message of appreciation that day.

Harriet Cornell, chairwoman of the Rockland County Legislature, gave the keynote address at the celebration. "People want food grown locally. The family farm offers healthy, sustainable choices to intelligent consumers," Cornell stated. "Many want to participate in growing food and have their children learn first-hand that food comes from the earth around us and not from the supermarket."

Paul Trader appeared at the anniversary on behalf of an institution that is celebrating its 150th anniversary: the land grant university system of which Cornell University is the representative in New York State. Created during the presidency of Abraham Lincoln, the system of publicly funded agricultural and technical institutions operates in every county of every state. Three generations of Concklins have graduated from Cornell.

"I first met the Concklin family in 1979 and have enjoyed working with them ever since," Trader, who is director of the Cornell Extension in Rockland County, told me on a recent phone interview. "Like most farmers, they understand what sustainable farming means in today's high-tech world. They've been tilling the same land for 300 years and using university research to grow healthy, delicious fruit and vegetables for their own farm stand in Pomona and almost 20 farmers' markets in our region."

When you shop at a farmers' market, you are helping reverse a trend that almost eliminated the family farm. The number of farms in the United States dropped from about seven million in the 1930s to only two million today. And only about one quarter of these remaining farms are family owned. Rockland County, once home to hundreds of farms, now has only a handful.

We need to acknowledge that saving the family farm is an act of self preservation. The more we become alienated from our food supply, the equilibrium of multiple systems that impact our lives is thrown off kilter. Agricultural policy affects our healthcare system through rising obesity rates; our environment through destructive practices of agribusiness that threaten our topsoil and the safety of our food supply; the enormous carbon footprint left by transporting produce over thousands of miles; and our economy through the loss of decent local jobs and the exorbitant prices that result from shipping food from outside our region.

Richard Concklin, the farm's managing partner, has personally greeted Farmers' Market shoppers in Nyack since the late 1980s. Richard's wife, Ellen, told me that without the farmers' market movement, their family farm would not be viable. But I think that the opposite view is equally valid. When you consider the urgent nutritional, environmental, and economic issues that are inextricably tied to our food supply, when you shop at a farmers' market, the family you save may be your own.

"The Orchards of Concklin is the oldest family business in New York State and the eighth oldest in the country."

2 South Mountain Road, Pomona, N.Y.

It's Bike Season, Be Safe

There were two dramatically different cycling events in Rockland County on May 19, 2013. Seven thousand cyclists rode through Nyack as part of the *Gran Fondo*, a competition that demonstrates the growing popularity of the sport. The other, a Ride of Silence on May 21, sponsored by the Rockland Bicycling Club, commemorated the injury and loss of life that happens too often when human and motor powered vehicles collide.

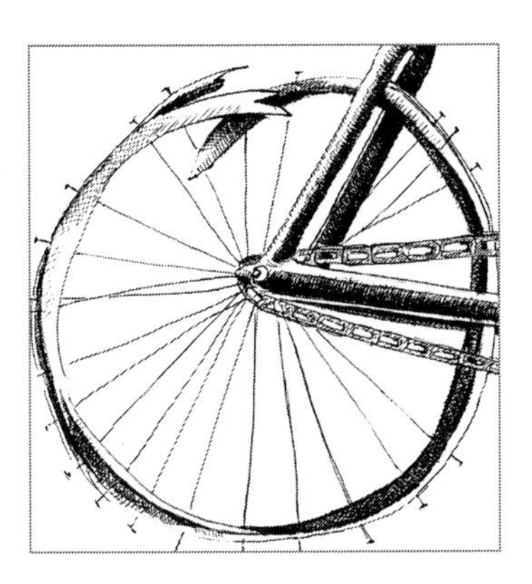

A steady stream of nearly 5,000 bikes passes through Nyack each weekend during the busiest part of the bicycle season. That's only 25 percent less than the total population of the village. Heidi Broecking, a local cycling enthusiast, believes that simple topography is a major reason the village is a popular destination on this two-wheel migration route. Broecking says if you want a long ride and you live in New York City you "gotta go north." "Route 9W is the easiest access point from the George Washington Bridge. Plus, we have beautiful river scenery, great hill climbing and interesting rest stops like Nyack, Piermont, and Haverstraw."

"A steady stream of nearly 5,000 bikes pass through Nyack each weekend during the busiest part of the bicycle season. That's only 25 percent less than the total population of the village."

When Broecking moved to Nyack 15 years ago, she saw fewer bikes on the road. Broecking reluctantly attributes the explosion in the number of cyclists to the sport's disgraced former champion. "Before Lance Armstrong, you wouldn't see 60 cyclists sitting outside the Runcible Spoon on North Broadway."

Broecking rapidly evolved from a recreational to semi-competitive cyclist. At first, she rode for fun with her son and husband, former Village of Nyack Trustee Steven Knowlton. "It was something that the three of us could do together without a babysitter. We bought a trailer that hitches on the back of the bike. It was a rolling living room. We would put our son, Devon, in there with juice, crackers, and toys. He would yell, 'Daddy, go faster.'"

But Heidi had a real need for speed and began to ride more seriously. She is now a member of the *Gruppo Sportivo*, an eight member ambassador team for *Gran Fondo* New York. A world-class event imported from Italy, the three-year-old *Gran Fondo New York* is a grueling 105-mile course, which starts at the George Washington Bridge, heads north along the Hudson River to Bear Mountain, and then turns south to finish in Weehawken, N.J. Broecking finished last month's event with a personal best time of seven hours and 20 minutes.

Whether riding competitively, for recreation, or just to get around town, peril is the constant companion of cyclists on our roads. On June 10, 2012, Pomona resident and recreational cyclist, Janet Martinez, was struck and killed by a car traveling south on Route 9W. "When you are wearing Lycra and a helmet and a driver is wearing two tons of metal, the cyclist doesn't have a chance," Broecking said.

In 2010, New York State enacted "Merrill's Law" to prevent tragedies like the accident that took the life of cycling advocate Merrill Cassell, who died from fatal injuries suffered after he was side-swiped by a bus in Westchester in 2009. Merrill's Law mandates that motorists must allow a safe distance when passing cyclists; three feet is recommended.

Celebrating 100 years
1909 2009
Sailing on the Hudson
BATSON '13

OCTOBER 15, 2013

Nyack Boat Club

Nyack Boat Club Commodore Kieran Quinn presided over his final Close of Season ceremony on October 27, 2013. His two-year term at the helm of the club, which concludes at year's end, included leading the effort to repair the wreckage wrought by Hurricane Sandy. Quinn, who served a shift of similar length as Mayor of Nyack from 1987 through 1990, reflects on issues that impact the club, the village, and the Hudson River and his fondness for "messing around in boats."

"Believe me, my young friend, there is NOTHING– absolutely nothing– half so much worth doing as simply messing about in boats."

When did you start boating?

As a child, I loved the water and boated a bit but my wife, Robin Brown, was much more of a boater than I. One of the reasons we moved to Nyack was to be near the Hudson. When we moved here in 1978, I learned to sail so Robin and I could sail together.

When did you join the Nyack Boat Club?

Robin and I joined Nyack Boat Club in 1980. As young marrieds, sailing was low-cost recreation. After we got home from work, we'd pack a sandwich, wedge our infant son's car seat into our little boat, and sail around the Tappan Zee.

Why is it a boat club and not a yacht club?

Nyack Boat Club was originally formed as a "do-it-yourself" boat club where members built and maintained the facilities to keep the cost of membership affordable. Being a "do-it-yourself" club continues to be an important part of our identity. We think we're the best sailing club on the Hudson, but we're resolutely a "boat club" not a "yacht club." In addition to the "do-it-yourself" ethos, the members see that their fellow members get the support they need to sail well and maintain their boats effectively. Additionally, we have an exceptionally strong sailing program for children.

How did Hurricane Sandy impact the club?

The winds, surge, storm-driven waves, and battering by storm-driven debris damaged the clubhouse, floating docks, piers, pilings, bulkheads, a fixed crane, hoisting machinery, electrical distribution equipment, club boats, pavement, and outdoor stairs and rails. We have restored most of the damaged facilities making them more storm resistant when practical.

Additionally, members lost boats at the Club and at boatyards where they had stored their boats for the winter. The physical repair is almost completed and we're on our way back financially. Some members have left, creating opportunities for others to join.

What benefits accrue to the Village from more recreational boating?

Currently, the village and surrounding area enjoys positive economic impact from the many who come to Nyack to boat. For example, recently 300 people from across the country and Canada participated in a three day regatta at Nyack Boat Club.

I understand this is your final year as Commodore. What is your fondest memory of your term in office?

I've enjoyed watching the young sailors learning responsibility, confidence, and independence through sailing, setting goals, and working to achieve them. It's gratifying to see families having fun together and to see our older sailors competing effectively against athletes one third their age. To quote from *The Wind in the Willows*, "Believe me, my young friend, there is NOTHING–absolutely nothing–half so much worth doing as simply messing about in boats."

Nyack Boat Club
59 Gedney Street, Nyack
nyackboatclub.org

N
E
S
West Gate
Cocktail Lounge

Best In More Ways Than One

Nyack has a family-owned and -operated hospitality business that will celebrate its 50th anniversary in 2015. Opened as the West Gate Motor Lodge because of its location on the western approach to the village, three generations labor to make the complex of buildings a popular center for resting, eating, and dancing. In 1989, the West Gate became a Best Western franchise, but the superlative "best" is more frequently used to describe their award-winning cheesecake and the salsa party they have thrown every Saturday night for over 30 years.

The family dynasty that has made desserts and dancing twin pillars of their motor lodge started in 1963 when Masis Parseghian bought the land known as the Nyack Ice Pond. Parseghian, a homebuilder, selected the land because of its proximity to a major highway and oversaw the construction of the original building and several expansions. American car culture fueled a demand for roadside motels to meet the basic needs of the traveling public, but in 1969, West Gate became more than a stopover. It was a destination.

In that year, the West Gate Restaurant and Lounge began serving and entertaining visitors. It started as a Polynesian restaurant and piano bar. In the early 1970s, it was called the Boom Boom Room. The club was located on the New York State Thruway, equidistant between Theater-Go-Rounds in Westchester and Rockland counties. Many of the A-list celebrities that played these massive venues used the Boom Boom Room as their after-hour hangout. According to sales manager and Parseghian's daughter, Lisa Dosch, Steve Lawrence and Eydie Gorme, Marlo Thomas, Steve Allen, and Ernie Kovacs would arrive after their local gigs had ended.

After a renovation in 1981, the elder Parseghian invited his friend and Rockland County resident, Tito Puente, to perform. The sold out appearance launched a major Latin music nightspot. For fifteen years, Puente performed several times a year. For the last 30 years, West Gate Lounge has been one of the most important night clubs for Salsa dancers and musicians in the tri-state area.

Lisa states there are several couples that fly in from Canada for weekend getaways built around the dance club. The international talent featured at the West Gate Lounge might explain the international patrons. The greatest names in Salsa music have taken the West Gate stage, including Eddie Palmerie, Johnny Pacheco, Jose Alberto, Eddie Torres, Tony Vega, and Eddie Santiago.

The dance floor is not Best Western's only recent claim to fame. Lisa Dosch's cheesecake has won first place in the New Jersey State Fair for two years in a row. Lisa learned her way around the kitchen from her mother and grandmother, but it was a customer's request for a new dessert menu item that led to her baking and serving her first cheesecake.

All four of Masis Parseghian's children now work side-by-side at West Gate. Her older brother, Gregory, is the General Manager; her brother, Jimmy, is Food and Beverage Manager; her sister, Donna Maccaro, manages the front desk operations. The hotel's founding father, who is 85, arrives at work almost daily at an establishment that now boasts 80 rooms, meeting spaces, and a banquet hall, in addition to the popular lounge and restaurant. "It feels like we are entertaining our guests from our home," says Lisa. "When you visit, it's our family meeting your family."

"As they prepare to celebrate their 50th year in 2015 as a family-owned and operated hospitality business, sweets for the stomach and salsa for the feet have made Best Western a culinary and cultural landmark."

26 Route 59, Nyack
westgatelounge.com

BATSON
10.27.12

One Poltergeist Place

As a matter of law, the house is haunted. This sentence, in a ruling by the New York State Supreme Court in July, 1991, generated international headlines for a real estate dispute surrounding the sale of 1 La Veta Place. That a court entertained the notion that a house could be haunted has kept the debate alive, especially on the arrival of a full moon and All Hallows' Eve. I recently collected the opinions of an informal jury of residents on La Veta, local realtors, and Rockland's own ghost investigator, Linda Zimmermann. Their unanimous verdict might surprise you.

"As a matter of law, the house is haunted."

Helen Ackley moved into the house at the end of La Veta Place in the early 1960s. The imposing Victorian was built around 1900 and had been used as both a single-family residence and a boarding house. Ackley, who shared the house with her children and grandchildren, reported to neighbors that her home was haunted. She described phantom footsteps, slamming doors, and beds being violently shaken. Even though the stories that she told were unnerving, the Ackleys described a peaceful co-existence with the spirits, who reportedly left gifts. According to Ackley, the disembodied visitors were a Revolutionary War-era couple, Sir George and Lady Margaret.

A neighbor who moved in a few doors down from 1 La Veta in the mid-80s was aware of the stories, but was always unconvinced. Any hint of skepticism did not stop Ackley from pitching her story to the media. Like any urban legend, the story grew with the oxygen of repetition and random events that seemed to buttress the original occult claim. When a relatively young and healthy guest at a dinner party at the Ackley home collapsed and died of a brain aneurysm, the story gained some creepy credence.

When Ackley decided to sell her home to Jeffrey Stambovsky in 1989, her ghost stories sank the sale. After making a deposit, Stambovsky learned 1 La Veta Place was on a tour of haunted properties. It was a fact that Ackley failed to mention to the prospective buyer. In Stambovsky v. Ackley, the New York State Supreme Court agreed with the buyer that he had the right to back out of the deal because Ackley didn't disclose any of the ghostly details.

The first person I approached to determine if the alleged apparitions existed was a former research chemist who has spent the last 15 years pursuing poltergeists as the Ghost Investigator. Linda Zimmermann came to ghost hunting by accident. "Local history was a hobby. But at the end of my lectures, people started asking about ghosts and inviting me to visit their homes."

I asked Zimmermann why La Veta Place had not made it on to her recently published list of the top 13 haunted sites in the Hudson Valley. You might think it would be in her interest as a ghost hunter to keep the legend of La Veta Place alive, but she was unimpressed. She told me that subsequent owners have reported no spectral sightings, something that current residents affirm.

After losing the court judgment, a disgusted Ackley moved to Florida. She was heard to declare that she was taking the ghosts with her. But the haunting of our popular culture creeps on. You might not believe in things that go bump in the night, but mere rumors of paranormal neighbors have created a genre that combines storytelling, history, and primordial fear, producing profits that are downright spooky.

8.11
BATSON
BATSON 8.1.11

Nyack Center

Nyack Center operates from the oldest surviving house of worship in our village, the First Presbyterian Church. The original sandstone building that stood on this spot was erected on land deeded by Peter Depew in 1816. It was torn down and replaced by today's familiar wooden edifice in 1839.

There is a life force emanating from the building that stands at Broadway and Depew Avenue, an aura from almost 200 years of uninterrupted community activity. If it were not for an enlightened congregation and a dynamic woman, this building would have been demolished in 1990.

Jane Sherman knew that a dwindling number of congregants could no longer sustain the church. As a Presbyterian elder and the head of Nyack's Park and Recreation committee, Sherman was also acutely aware of the need for space for young people in the community. Finding herself at the intersection of need and opportunity, Sherman was able to convince the Presbytery of New York to confer the church property to a nonprofit for $1.

A less principled religious body would have been happy to sell this prime parcel to a real estate developer. Instead, they embraced the piety of allowing the not-for-profit function of this property to endure. In response to Sherman's bold gesture, the community stepped forward to help secure this legacy by donating funds and volunteering labor—people like Jo and Peter Baer, who made substantial contributions to help transform a 19th-century church into a 21st-century community center. The task of continuing the epic tradition of good works at the site now falls on the skilled shoulders of Kim Cross, Executive Director of the Nyack Center.

The entire community is a stakeholder in the future of Nyack Center. The building houses celebrated art programs like Rivertown Films. Important civic institutions, including the NAACP and Gay Pride of Rockland, use the facility for meetings and special events. There is no other venue that has both the capacity and the mandate to open its doors to every segment of the community, sometimes at a moment's notice.

My drawing exaggerates the posture of the structure. The top tier looks like a soggy wedding cake in my sketch. Brooke Malloy and Nicole Hines, Assistant Director and Office Manager, respectively, of Nyack Center were kind enough to humor me on a recent visit. They allowed me to climb a vertical ladder into the bell tower. On my request, Brooke rang the bell. Chiming at 1:35pm on a Friday, a few people must have double-checked their watches. But in another century, a bell that tolled on an irregular interval was a warning or a call to arms.

Our country was only 63 years old when the cornerstone was laid for this building. Scores of generations have maintained this fragile wooden structure through weekly offerings, charitable donations, and public revenue.

Consider donating to Nyack Center, as so many have before you. Contribute money or volunteer, attend an event, or write a letter of support. Let's make sure that Nyack Center is alive and well in 2039 when this special building celebrates its 200th birthday.

"Scores of generations have maintained this fragile wooden structure through weekly offerings, charitable donations and public revenue."

58 Depew Ave, Nyack
nyackcenter.org

Brave New Normal

On a recent phone call with President Barack Obama, New York Governor Andrew Cuomo observed that we seem to have a one hundred year storm every year now. There is a compelling truth in Cuomo's jest. With each storm season, the eventuality of power outages is becoming more certain and the duration of the outages is getting longer. Welcome to the brave new normal.

"With each storm season, the eventuality of power outages is becoming more certain and the duration of the outages is getting longer. Welcome to the brave new normal."

Utilities, like Orange & Rockland, need to demonstrate to consumers and public officials that they can cope with a one hundred year storm every year. If utilities need funds to update their infrastructure, or even radically change the delivery system, like burying power lines as New York City did after the lethal blizzard of 1888, then they need to put those costs on the table. The alternative is just as costly. Can our public health and safety and our economy survive a yearly two-week power disruption? Since O & R has a monopoly on delivering electricity, the legislature needs to find a way, through either incentive-based or punitive measures, to demand the improvements that competitive corporations must undertake.

Gas stations should be required to install generators so they can continue to distribute fuel when power disruptions occur. Even though post-Sandy fuel shortages resulted from barges being unable to off-load shipments, stations that had fuel and could not pump because they lacked electricity exacerbated the early stages of the problem.

Institutions that depend on generators, like hospitals and water treatment plants, need to have protocols to ensure they can continue to operate on generator power for a least a month in the event that the portion of the electrical grid that they rely on is destroyed and must be rebuilt.

With the prospect of future "super" storms, a new protocol of personal responsibility is also in order. Having a "go bag" is no longer sufficient. We need to stage giant "stay bags." People now need to assemble enough provisions to shelter-in-place for at least two weeks. And since there are many in our community without the personal, physical, and financial wherewithal to accumulate sufficient supplies, we need to develop a data base of the elderly and infirm on a community-by-community basis so that when storms hit, we can systematically reach out to these at-risk individuals. Yes, we need to be able to take care of ourselves when governments and utilities cannot supply a secure and uninterrupted power supply, but I don't think any of us want to concede survival in a crisis should be an every-man-for-himself affair.

We should also try to develop some indoor alternatives to Halloween, like the Monster Mash that Nyack Center throws every year, because it seems as though Mother Nature likes to send tricks, and not treats, every late October.

Governor Cuomo argued on the Rachel Maddow Show, that we may not be able to agree on the cause of extreme weather, but the harmful effects of these events are inarguable. As residents of a river village in a coastal region, we need to get serious about storm preparedness. For those who attended any of the daily emergency town hall meetings at 11:00am at Village Hall, the indomitable spirit of our community that was on display is this storm's silver lining. We need to bank some of that silver, because there are storm clouds gathering on the horizon.

This week's sketch is of the remains of the houseboat owned by Jerry Donnellan, director of the County of Rockland Veterans Service Agency.

VCS GAY PRIDE Rockland
Sunday, June 8 ~ Riverspace Parking Lot, Nyack

JUNE 3, 2014

Gay Pride Rockland

In 1999, over 1,000 people gathered for the first Gay Pride event in Nyack. As if to prove the positive force that this public affirmation of sexual identity can have, Village of Nyack trustee John Shields, who later served four terms as Mayor, publicly came out of the closet that day. This pioneering local Gay Pride celebration will be held this Sunday.

In the late 1990s, if you lived in Nyack and wanted to attend one of the major Gay Pride celebrations that are held around the country each June, you had to travel to Manhattan. Phyllis B. Frank, Associate Executive Director of VCS Inc., enjoyed the annual pride pilgrimage to the city, but thought aloud to others that "even if we had just a group walking behind one sign, we needed to do something for Gay Pride here in Rockland."

This year's celebration comes at a time when countervailing global social currents reverberate through the gay rights arena. On May 21, a federal judge in Michigan declared that state's ban on gay marriage was unconstitutional, bringing the number of states where gay marriage is legal to 19. However, governments in nations such as Russia and Uganda have passed laws that practically make it illegal to be gay. In Uganda, sanctions include the death penalty.

Gay Pride celebrations are held throughout the world this month to commemorate protests that followed a raid by New York City Police officers on Stonewall Inn on June 28, 1969. The uprising in Greenwich Village against a pattern and practice of harassment by public officials is widely regarded as the beginning of the Gay Rights Movement.

Since 1970, VCS Inc. has developed programs to confront heterosexism, homophobia, and transphobia, racism and sexism, with a particular focus on violence against women. A social justice thread is woven into the fabric of the work of VCS. The first words on their website describe the organization as "a family service agency with an anti-racist, social justice mission."

Phyllis Frank joined VCS in 1974. Under her leadership, VCS has developed a wide range of LGBT family services, support programs, and professional training, including evolving expertise in relation to transgender children, youth, and adults. Her exemplary efforts resulted in her being inducted into the Rockland County Civil Rights Hall of Fame in 2012.

The premise behind VCS is that community lay people can provide high level counseling for clients with a wide range of serious social problems. The model called "Volunteer Family Counseling Project" was initiated by Dr. Stephen Shapiro and Martin Eisman of the Family Service Association of Rockland County and funded by The Ford Foundation in 1970. The first group of 16 volunteers were recruited, trained, and assigned to work with 34 families. The program quickly expanded to 426 families and individuals assisted by 108 trained volunteers. Later that year, the agency moved into offices at 151 South Main Street in New City.

Over 40 years later, VCS provides an array of services, including child abuse prevention programs, services to older adults and their families, and low cost counseling to Rockland residents for a variety of life issues, such as separation, co-parenting children, unemployment, and domestic violence. VCS conducts a widely acclaimed counselor training program, administers a nationally recognized New York Model for Batterer Programs, a federally supported Foster Grandparent program, and various social justice programs, including Gay Pride Rockland.

"Even if we had just a group walking behind one sign, we needed to do something for Gay Pride here in Rockland." Phyllis B. Frank, Associate Executive Director of VCS, Inc.

77 South Main Street
New City, N.Y.
vcs-inc.org

BATSON 9-28-12

Amazing Grace Circus

Amazing Grace Circus! is a youth organization formed after the tragic events of September 11th. The arts and fitness initiative helped local youth heal and express their feelings, frustrations, and fears after losing loved ones in the community. Here is how a program that sends the spirits of young people soaring, sprang from the emotional abyss that followed the attack on Lower Manhattan.

A group of young people at Grace Episcopal Church sought a way to comprehend the enormity of the violent event and the personal loss of members of their church community, Welles Remy Crowther and Stacey Sennas McGowan. In their search for solace, they founded a circus.

The teens were already part of the Grace Episcopal Church's Senior Youth Group chaperoned by Carlo Pellegrini and Janet Hayes, a group that Crowther's sister, Paige, had attended. Pellegrini, a veteran circus performer and dancer, had introduced some basic circus skills as team and esteem building activities. Hayes brought her experience as a licensed occupational therapy assistant to facilitate eight months of workshops.

"One day the teens took Janet and me to what was then the Skylark Diner, the restaurant now known as Johnny Cakes. They had something to tell us," Pellegrini recalled. "We are teenagers, therefore we are amazing. And we are at Grace Church, that makes us the Amazing Grace Circus," the kids declared.

Pellegrini needed some convincing at first. Having spent a year of traveling the country as a member of the Royal Lichtenstein Quarter Ring Sidewalk Circus in the early 70s, he knew the demands of the art form. But the young people would not take no for an answer. Thanks to their persistence, and sublime and resilient response to tragedy, during the last ten years over 100 teens have been members of the troupe and approximately 30,000 young people and families have witnessed and been inspired by Amazing Grace Circus! performances.

Two other adults have brought their talents to help Amazing Grace Circus! performers tumble, juggle, clown, and soar. Karen Gersch, a founding member of the Big Apple Circus and visual artist, teaches acrobatics and clowning. Hilary Sweeney, a ballet dancer since the age of five, who has trained with some of the leading aerial artists in the field, has taught dance, silks, and trapeze.

Pellegrini believes that eventually, youth circus will be as ubiquitous as youth soccer. Growing interest in three-ring recreational arts and sports could be the outgrowth of the mass appeal of Cirque Du Soleil, the Canadian-based company that stages year-round performances in New York City and Las Vegas. Twenty years ago there were only three youth circuses in the country, now there are 140.

The arts and fitness program at Amazing Grace Circus! prepares young people for success in acrobatics and academics. Alum Kenneth Lindemann won a coveted spot in the Seven Digits circus troupe in Montreal and troupe members Adam Kapilow and Katherine Geber were accepted by Swarthmore and Oberlin colleges respectively.

In circus custom, before a troupe toured the countryside, they were blessed by a church figure. By chance, an Episcopal Bishop was on hand before Amazing Grace's first performance in 2002 to perform the rite. But when you consider that this phenomenal and enduring program was the brainchild of young people responding to one of the darkest moments in American history, we are all the recipients of the blessing that is Amazing Grace Circus!

"A program that sends the spirits of young people soaring, sprang from the emotional abyss that followed the attack on Lower Manhattan."

Grace Church is located at 130 1st Avenue, Nyack.

PEACE

Fellowship of Reconciliation

"This is the house where Martin Luther King would have slept."

This is the house where Martin Luther King, Jr. would have slept. Were it not for an assassin in Memphis in 1968, our nation's Nobel Peace Prize-winning champion of nonviolence would have made it to Nyack. The purpose of his visit would have been to commune with the Fellowship of Reconciliation, an organization that shared his philosophy and stood with him during his defining struggle.

Since its founding in 1914, the Fellowship of Reconciliation (FOR) has been a global emissary for peace among people and nations. Befitting their humanitarian imperative, the organization was founded on a handshake between two men, Henry Hodgkin, an English Quaker, and Friedrich Sigmund-Schultze, a German Lutheran, whose countries had just declared war on each other. They were attending a conference of religious leaders that sought to prevent the conflict that would engulf the world and vowed to work together for peace, even though their countries were at war. Succeeding generations of FOR members have kept that pledge.

Today, FOR is engaged in peace missions throughout the world through task forces on social, economic, and racial justice in the United States, Latin America, the Caribbean, and the Middle East. FOR's commitment to demilitarization is absolute. As an organization, they were instrumental in establishing the legal recognition for conscientious objector status before World War II. Richard Deats, their past Executive Secretary, describes the organization's philosophy as the belief that truth is stronger than falsehood, love overcomes hate, and nonviolence is more enduring than violence.

When Texas minister and FOR staffer, Reverend Glenn Smiley, first encountered Dr. King in Montgomery, Alabama, in 1955, their handshake honored and echoed the gesture on the train platform in Cologne, Germany, that launched FOR. The Montgomery bus boycott that King led was viewed by the white establishment of the south as a declaration of war. FOR sent Smiley to meet with King to find a nonviolent solution to the looming conflict between the races in the American South, a mission hauntingly similar to the goal of the ecumenical conference in Germany prior to World War I.

Smiley was encouraged to learn that King had heard of the tactics of civil disobedience that Mahatma Gandhi had used to end British colonial rule in India. Smiley, and another FOR staffer, who would become a longtime King associate, Bayard Rustin, assisted in conducting workshops to inculcate the spirit of nonviolence in a conflict that would require the black community to endure insults, beatings, imprisonment, and bombings.

The story of the boycott is recorded in a very special comic book that FOR has recently re-released. Originally published in 1958, the volume chronicles the 381-day bus boycott that led to the eventual collapse of Jim Crow laws in the South. The comic, produced by a bullpen of artists under the supervision of popular cartoonist, Al Capp, in New York, is a testimonial to the courage and humanity of the people of Montgomery. It is also a primer on nonviolent direct action. More importantly, it has become a vessel for the teachings of King to endure. Dalia Ziada, formerly the Cairo-based North Africa Director of the American Islamic Congress, translated the comic into Arabic and Farsi several years ago and distributed thousands of copies from Yemen to Morocco. Copies of the illustrated history of the Montgomery bus boycott were circulated in Tahrir Square in Cairo in February 2011.

521 N. Broadway, Nyack
forusa.org

Two Row Wampum

The Two Row Wampum paddle was organized through a partnership between the Onondaga Nation and Neighbors of the Onondaga Nation (NOON) as part of a statewide educational campaign to commemorate the 400th anniversary of the first treaty between the Haudenosaunee (also known as the Iroquois) and European settlers. On August 9, 2013, the Two Row Wampum Renewal Campaign will land on and march across Manhattan Island to the United Nations to participate in the International Day of the World's Indigenous Peoples.

To this day, the Haudenosaunee retain the Two Row Wampum belt on which this treaty was originally recorded. Approximately 150 boats launched from Rensselaer, N.Y., on July 28 for the 13-day trip to New York City. The flotilla will paddle between nine and 15 miles each day and camp along the Hudson River route.

Dwaine Perry, Chief of the Ramapough Lunaape, will meet the floating delegation as they overnight in Piermont. Chief Perry is taking the opportunity of the flotilla's arrival in Rockland County to remind the river villages of the central role that Native American people played in the creation of this nation: "I would like people to know that without the aid of the Ramapough Lunaape there would not have been a Lexington and Concord, nor an American Revolution as we know it," he explained.

"When George Washington was a Captain and Alexander Hamilton was a lieutenant working in the Ramapo Pass, our ancestors allowed them the use of the strategic route, which was then a choke point and the only way into the colonies from the North with any meaningful troop levels."

According to Chief Perry, the first 900 cannonballs used in the American Revolution were produced from the Lunaape Mines in Ringwood. The fabled "Chain across the Hudson" was made from their iron. "Yet those who have created the greatest nation on earth have failed to acknowledge the people who have made this grand experiment possible," he continued.

The goals of the Two Row Wampum Renewal Campaigns are described as a three-part vision of peace, friendship, and a sustainable future in parallel forever. The choice of using the Hudson River (known as the Muhheakantuck, or the Great Mohegan by the Iroquois, and "the river that flows both ways" by the Lunaape), as the conveyance to take the original treaty to an international summit is potent with symbolism that reinforces these goals.

The river that these canoes navigate was silent witness to the original treaty that is recorded on the Two Row Wampum that the flotilla carries. The act of paddling, with boats joining along the way and camping in various river communities, allows native and non-natives to create new and deepen old relationships. And as we are all inextricably entwined by the fate of the river, the Hudson is the ideal locus and focus for the campaign's events. "It is hoped the Two Row Wampum Campaign will heighten the understanding for the urgency of increased environmental awareness. The need for mutual respect of both human beings and the environment is crucial to the overall quality of life and survivability of the planet. Water is the blood of our grandmother, Earth. Without clean water, we all will perish. Without the nurturing of the environment, the essence of all life, man will be diminished correspondingly and without exception," Chief Perry said.

"I would like people to know that without the aide of the Ramapough Lunaape there would not have been a Lexington and Concord nor an American Revolution as we know it." Dwaine Perry, Chief of the Ramapough Lunaape.

ramapoughlenapenation.org

Franklin Antiques
140 MAIN STREET
NYACK TOBACCO COMPANY
FOR LEASE
Main St
Franklin St

OCTOBER 11, 2011

Sketch Log vs. Google Maps

"I'll need one hundred John Henrys to create a handmade version of the Google Street View map."

Like John Henry, I am at war with a machine. My antagonist is not a steam-powered drill, but Google Maps. What my nemesis accomplishes through satellite surveillance and cars equipped with periscope cameras, I endeavor to create with my humble sketchpad and pen. My comprehensive visual record of every inch, object, vista, and structure in my village will remind us that handmade, no matter how much slower, shakier, or flawed, has a greater intrinsic value than the synthetic alternative.

Perfection is overrated. When my mother had a set of teeth made for herself recently, the dentist warned that the final mold had to be imperfect. If a dental implant is composed of teeth that are too symmetrical, the human eye senses that they are false teeth.

Are machines weakening humans? During the summer you can see people using mechanical equipment to groom their yards and gardens, hogging energy that is not renewable, and ignoring an excellent opportunity to engage in some cardio. If you drew a bar graph describing the shortening of the attention span of modern man, how steep a line would you have to draw to connect the handwritten letter to Twitter?

In a culture where machines do the physical work, will people become soft? In an era when machines perform all the mental work, will people become vapid? Could we reach a point in our society where we become as dependent on our machines as a critically ill patient is on life support? What would happen if our plug gets pulled? Will the dynamic eventually shift, making the machine the operator and the human the tool?

Some cultures view machines with suspicion and seem intrinsically aware of the limits of mechanical reproduction. When you attempt to use a camera to take a picture of a person in some parts of the world, you risk an indignant assault. Some cultures view the mechanical lens as at best an intrusive instrument, at worst a soul thieving contraption. But when you approach the very same party with a sketch pad, the results are radically different.

In a Masai village in Kenya, the act of sketching created two crowds, one watching me draw, the other waiting to pose. When I started the *Nyack Sketch Log*, I thought that I would get run off peoples' front lawns as a trespasser or suspected peeping tom. But, like my experience in Kenya, the opposite has been true. The act of drawing from life seems to soothe the jumpy modern soul.

Every structure that I record, manually, through my sketch log was constructed by human hands. Handcraftsmanship imparts a human spirit into an object. The absence of the human hand is what makes Google Maps a relative of the steam-powered drill of John Henry legend and, henceforth, my adversary. The Google Map will always be superior to my super-sized sketch log as a navigation tool. But as an archive of our collective time on the planet, I believe the artistic record reigns supreme.

Upon reflection, one artist alone can hardly record a village that is one square mile in size. One John Henry will not be enough. I'll need one hundred John Henrys to create a handmade version of the Google Street View map.

Nyack News & Views

NYACK SKETCH LOG APPEARS EVERY TUESDAY ON NYACKNEWSANDVIEWS.COM

Since 2007, *NyackNewsAndViews* has published original news, opinion, and cultural content daily about the Nyack river villages.

Acknowledgments

MY FAMILY

My mother, Daisy Batson, for exposing me to art at an early age.
My cousin and business partner, Sylvia Peterson.
Janae Peterson, my naughter (niece + daughter), a constant source of inspiration.

NYACK SKETCH LOG BOOK PRODUCTION TEAM

Sabrina Weld Feldman, Sponsor
James Hershberger, Project Manager
Loraine Machlin, Designer
Pat Jarden, Copy Editor
Nancy Eisen, Troubleshooter
Special thanks to Judy Martin, the earliest supporter for this project, who proofread every essay twice, once before online publication and again for the book.

I WISH TO THANK THE FOLLOWING INDIVIDUALS FOR HELPING ME PUBLISH THIS COLLECTION OF SKETCHES AND SHORT ESSAYS.

Scott Baird, Erin Bekowies, David e. Bell, Ross Meckler Benjamin, Kris Burns, Barbara Caress, Reuden Chase, Art Clark, Loreen Costa, Jeff Doctorow, Jack Dunnigan, Nancy Eisen, Dorothea Erichsen, Betsey Franco Feeny, Sabrina Weld Feldman, Peter Fruchtman, Craig Gordon, John Gromada, Art Gunther III, Janet Hamlin, Ben Harwood, Howard Hellman, James Hershberger, Victoria Hertz, Cynthia Imperatore, Bill Irwin, Pat Jarden, Brian Jennings, Jim Katzenstein, Tracy Kachtick Anders, Wesley King, Frank LoBuono, Rachel Mack, Loraine Machlin, Judy Martin, Dr. Lori Martin, Enid Mastrianni, Jennifer McCann, Joyce Molnar, Pam Moskowitz, Dane Paciarello, Hal Parker, Carlo Pellegrini, Carole Perry, Win and Betty Perry, Janae Peterson, Sylvia Peterson, Dr. Arnold Roufa, Jennifer Rothschild, Rosemary Serluca, John Shields, Skye O'Jea Spiegel, Laura Straus, Myra Starr, Janey Tannenbaum, Rick Tannenbaum, Bonnie Sherlock Timm, Jen Laird-White, Maria Luisa Whittingham, Valerie Wolzien, Ray Wright, Dave Zornow.

NYACK SKETCH LOG COLUMN PRODUCTION TEAM

Nyack Sketch Log appears every Tuesday on *NyackNewsAndViews.com*. Without the assistance of the following individuals and institutions, I could not have produced a weekly sketch and short essay for the last three years.

Paul Adler, Susan Roth-Beerman, Philip Biagioli, Rev. Isidoa Branch Jr., Kris Burns, Bill Coughlin, Kim Cross, Jerry Donnellan, Jack Dunnigan, Nancy Eisen, Alan Englander, Marianne and Jan Faust, Evelyn Fitzgerald, Courtney George, Bob Goldberg, Art Gunther III, Matt Haviland, Doria Hillsman, Michael Houghton, Brian Jennings, Jerry Koblin, Barry Koch, Mia Leo, Carolyn Magnani, John Papastathis, Win and Betty Perry, Brooke Malloy, Lee Mamunes, Judy Martin, Dr. Lori Martin, Pam Moskowitz, Alma Richmond, Richard Quinn, Matthew Seig, John Shields, John Patrick Schutz, Sam Smith, Myra Starr, Gini Stolldorf, Leontine Temsky, Diana Wilkins, Carol Weiss, Dave Zornow, co-founder, *NyackNewsAndViews.com*.

Historical Society of the Nyacks, Nyack Library, Edward Hopper House Arts Center.

SEVERAL OF MY SOURCES OR SUBJECTS ARE NO LONGER WITH US, BUT THEY LIVE ON THROUGH THEIR CONTRIBUTIONS TO THIS VILLAGE.

Edwin Azanedo 1955-2013
Frances A. Batson 1920-2009
William Prime Batson 1921-2013
LeRoy Gates 1902-1972
Jacqueline L. Holland 1925-2007
Hazel P. Lancaster 1924-2014
Virginia Parkhurst 1878-1965

Photo: Ray Wright

About the Author

Bill Batson has published a sketch and short essay about the village every week since August 2011 on *NyackNewsAndViews.com*. His family has been in Nyack since 1890. Bill also serves as the artist-in-residence at the Nyack Farmers' Market, where he sells art, organizes entertainment and develops promotional tools for the Chamber of Commerce. A lifelong artist and activist, Bill is dedicated to using the visual arts to promote preservation, cultural education and community empowerment.

To learn more about Bill's work and to follow his weekly column, visit billbatsonarts.com.